Urban Education

URBAN STUDIES INFORMATION GUIDE SERIES

Series Editor: Thomas P. Murphy, Director, Institute for Urban Studies at the University of Maryland, College Park (on leave) and Director of the Federal Executive Institute, Charlottesville, Virginia

Also in this series:

SUBURBIA—*Edited by Joseph Zikmund II and Deborah Ellis Dennis**

URBAN COMMUNITY—*Edited by Anthony J. Filipovitch and Earl J. Reeves*

URBAN DECISION MAKING: THE BASIS FOR ANALYSIS—*Edited by Mark Drucker**

URBAN FISCAL POLICY AND ADMINISTRATION—*Edited by John L. Mikesell and Jerry L. McCaffery**

URBAN HOUSING: PUBLIC AND PRIVATE—*Edited by John E. Rouse, Jr.*

URBAN INDICATORS—*Edited by Thomas P. Murphy**

URBAN LAW—*Edited by Robert D. Kline and Thomas P. Murphy**

URBAN MANAGEMENT—*Edited by Bernard H. Ross**

URBAN PLANNING—*Edited by Ernest R. Alexander, Anthony J. Catanese, and David S. Sawicki*

URBAN POLICY—*Edited by Dennis J. Palumbo and George Taylor*

URBAN POLITICS—*Edited by Thomas P. Murphy*

WOMEN AND URBAN SOCIETY—*Edited by Hasia R. Diner*

*in preparation

The above series is part of the

GALE INFORMATION GUIDE LIBRARY

The Library consists of a number of separate series of guides covering major areas in the social sciences, humanities, and current affairs.

General Editor: Paul Wasserman, Professor and former Dean, School of Library and Information Services, University of Maryland

Managing Editor: Denise Allard Adzigian, Gale Research Company

Urban Education

A GUIDE TO INFORMATION SOURCES

Volume 3 in the Urban Studies Information Guide Series

George E. Spear

*Associate Dean of Continuing Education
and
Associate Professor, School of Education
University of Missouri-Kansas City*

Donald W. Mocker

*Associate Professor of Education
University of Missouri-Kansas City*

Gale Research Company
Book Tower, Detroit, Michigan 48226

50350

Library of Congress Cataloging in Publication Data

Spear, George E
    Urban education.

    (Urban studies information guide series ; v. 3)
    Includes indexes.
  1. Education, Urban--United States. I. Mocker,
Donald W., joint author. II. Title. III. Series.
LC5131.M55   370.19'348'0973   78-13627
ISBN 0-8103-1431-2

50350

VITAE

George E. Spear is associate dean for Continuing Education and associate professor in the School of Education, University of Missouri-Kansas City. He was director of the Center for Resource Development in Adult Education, served three years as associate dean in the Division for Continuing Education at University of Missouri-Kansas City, and teaches courses in adult education.

Spear received his B.A. from Baker University, M.A. from the University of Missouri-Kansas City, and Ph.D. from the University of Michigan. He is a former journalist and a fellow in the Mott Foundation Inter-University Clinical Preparation Program in community education, Flint, Michigan. He is a codeveloper of the Master of Arts degree in Adult and Continuing Education, University of Missouri-Kansas City.

Donald W. Mocker is an associate professor of education at the University of Missouri-Kansas City where he teaches in the areas of curriculum and adult education. He served as associate director of the Center for Resource Development in Adult Education, 1973-76, and developed a seminal work dealing with teacher competencies in adult education.

Mocker received his B.S. from Missouri Valley College, M.S. from the University of Missouri-Columbia, and Ed.D. from the State University of New York-Albany. He is a frequent contributor to journals devoted to adult education and is a consultant in the areas of adult reading, and program and instructional planning. He is a codeveloper of the Master of Arts degree in Adult and Continuing Education, University of Missouri-Kansas City.

CONTENTS

INTRODUCTION

"Every man in America thinks he could run a filling station and a school better than the people who are doing it now." This observation by a colleague some twenty years ago spotlights one of two major problems which beset the editors in assembling the bibliographical content of this volume on urban education. Few fields of endeavor are so blessed as is education with so many experts ranging from federal judges to truck drivers, nuclear submariners to housewives, college professors to functional illiterates. The result is a continuing flood of literature that inundates the highlands and lowlands of the field with books, articles, studies, and reports making the selection of the useful from the useless a tedious and arduous task.

The second problem stems from the difficulty in identifying the meaning and significance of the description "urban." Significant numbers of urban-specific writings began appearing in 1967-68 and the majority of listings here are products of the present decade. EDUCATION INDEX, for example, did not list urban education as a category until the 1969-70 edition, having referred searchers to "city" or "municipal" headings prior to that volume. This volume reflects that general state of the literature with only a scattering of references predating 1966.

Urbanism as a complex social concept was not widely recognized until the mid-1960s; there were no urban educators, urban economists, urban anthropologists, or urban planners. In the past decade, however, this nation has firmly identified itself as an urban rather than agrarian society, and it is increasingly difficult to select from the volumes of literature those pieces that are peculiarly urban in character as opposed to those of a more general societal nature.

Given the above problems, the task of compiling this volume has called for selective judgment in the choice of resources listed here. This judgment was based both on professional experience and extensive consultations with respected educators across the country.

It was viewed as useful to abandon traditional index categories in favor of a problem-centered format based on contemporary issues and problems in the major areas under which education is generally organized and addressed. Those three macrocategories are: part I—Preschool, Elementary, Secondary Schools—that segment of education dealing with initial socialization and preparation for life; part II—Urban Higher Education—advanced academic and professional preparation; and part III—Adult Education—lifelong learning for adaptation to and enrichment of the adult years.

Part I identifies changes in location and characteristics of population, improvement of instruction, teacher training, community control, and the future of education in the urban environment as the major issues and questions facing those concerned primarily with the education of youth.

Part II highlights the new demands of the urban society upon higher education to break with some of its tradition and to be accountable for life in the world around it. Specifically this part deals with nontraditional programs and degrees, citizen involvement, urban minorities, and staff training for meeting these urban requirements.

Part III addresses the new and rapidly growing concern for lifelong learning as a demand upon both the individual, and institutions and agencies within the urban community. Financing of adult education is one of the major areas of concern since traditional resources are seldom available to adult education. Further attention then is given to recruitment and participation of adult learners, curriculum development to meet special adult needs, and to the interaction and interdependence among the variety of agencies that address the learning needs and interests of the adult population.

It is the intent of this volume to serve the resource needs of professional educators, students, and a concerned citizenry which at once is responsible for and must be served by the total educational enterprise.

The reader should note that the many individual listings containing code numbers, such as "ED 073 902," are available through the system of Educational Resources Information Centers (ERIC). Most moderate to large public libraries, colleges and universities, and state departments of education have their complete files on microfiche along with directories and detailed information on utilizing the system's various reference services.

We gratefully acknowledge the valuable assistance of Georgia Girardeau and Elizabeth Noble in compiling the contents of this work, and Brenda Fasken in preparation of the manuscript.

George E. Spear
Donald W. Mocker

Part I
PRESCHOOL, ELEMENTARY, AND
SECONDARY SCHOOLS

An aroused public conscience in the United States in the 1960s mandated a vigorous attack on social and economic inequities and it decided the battle-ground would be in American cities where the faults were painfully visible, increasingly emotional, and potentially disruptive. This new kind of war also sowed the seeds for the development of an awareness that this had become an urban rather than an agrarian society.

With an untested faith in its educational system as a major force for change, the nation looked to its schools to provide not only the foundations of knowledge and skills to its children, but also to solve many of the historic, social, and cultural dilemmas among its people.

Rising expectations for the new era called for new understanding about the problems of urban life. How should school programs be revised to meet these problems? What should be done to prepare teachers to meet these challenges and demands? A doctrine of maximum feasible participation in all community affairs raised issues of control and responsiveness which were foreign to the traditional assumptions of educators at all levels.

Part I addresses the issues and circumstances affecting these foundations of American education. It reports on a variety of efforts by the educational system to change and to accommodate new expectations and goals. Much of what was tried, whether success or failure, helped the nation become more educationally aware. This material is presented here to provide an overview of education in a major period of transition, and to consider future directions for urban education.

Section A

CHANGING POPULATION PATTERNS IN URBAN AREAS

Bowles, Gladys K., et al. POVERTY DIMENSIONS OF RURAL-TO-URBAN MIGRATION: A STATISTICAL REPORT. POPULATION-MIGRATION REPORTS, RURAL-URBAN MIGRANTS. Vol. 1, pt. 1. Washington, D.C.: Superintendent of Documents, Government Printing Office, 1973. (ED 073 902)

> Statistics systematized from the 1967 Survey of Economic Opportunity for a study of the poverty dimensions of rural-to-urban migration are presented in this report. The data presented in the tables were collected by the Bureau of the Census.

EDUCATIONAL FACILITIES IN THE PENSACOLA METROPOLITAN AREA. Pensacola, Fla.: Escambia-Santa Rosa Regional Planning Council, 1970.

> The report inventories all existing and proposed school facilities in the Pensacola metropolitan area, and identifies those facilities that are likely to be abandoned in the future. Immediate and short-term needs are identified, including the estimated cost of facilities. Long-range needs are also considered.

Green, Robert L., and Pettigrew, Thomas F. "Urban Desegregation and White Flight: A Response to Coleman." PHI DELTA KAPPAN 57 (February 1976): 399-402.

> The authors discuss issues raised by James S. Coleman's latest research. They concluded that the research is questionable, that only a tenuous connection exists between it and Coleman's anti-busing "political" opinions, and that social scientists generally should not debate policy implications of their research findings in the mass media.

Lombardi, John. "Unique Problems of the Inner City Colleges." Speech presented to the California Junior College Association, Anaheim, California, 31 October 1968. (ED 026 057)

> This speech deals with the way in which urban changes such as population increase, shifts in population groups, suburban growth,

3

and central city decay have produced special problems for the inner-city college such as de facto segregation, inadequate education programs, racial imbalance of employees, and participant activities.

Mason, Robert E. "Decline and Crisis in Big-City Education." PHI DELTA KAPPAN 48 (March 1967): 303-10. (ED 020 265)

Current population trends have created vast educational problems in large urban centers. While thousands of low-income Puerto Ricans and Negroes have migrated to central-city areas, white middle-class persons and expanding industries continue to relocate in the suburbs.

PLANNING FOR CHANGE. New York: Hatch C. Richard Associates, 1968. (ED 069 621)

This workbook is designed to enable the New York public school student to gather and structure information on the history, condition, and function of their neighborhoods. Following an introduction, the material describes reasons for migration into the city, characteristics of the neighborhood, and practical and utopian alternatives.

RENSSELAER COUNTY POPULATION: ANALYSIS 1968: PROJECTION 1990. Troy, N.Y.: Rensselaer County Department of Planning and Promotion, 1969.

This report contains population growth, metropolitan trends, population changes, population density, composition of the population, selected population characteristics, and estimates of future population.

U. S. Department of Commerce. Bureau of the Census. CENSUS OF POPULATION: 1970. SUBJECT REPORTS. MOBILITY FOR METROPOLITAN AREAS. Washington, D.C.: 1970.

The statistics in this report provide information on the movement of persons five years old and over to, from, and within the standard metropolitan statistical areas of the United States during the period 1965 to 1970.

_____. CONSUMER INCOME. Current Population Reports, Special Studies Series P-60, No. 101. Washington, D.C.: 1976.

Education and employment statistics, in conjunction with population patterns--urban and nonurban, are provided. Trends in family income are detailed by demographic characteristics.

_____. CURRENT POPULATION REPORTS. SPECIAL STUDIES. SOME DEMOGRAPHIC ASPECTS OF AGING IN THE UNITED STATES, 1973. Washington, D.C.: 1973.

This report presents some demographic aspects of aging in the United States. It focuses on the demographic characteristics of older persons, namely those over fifty-five, particularly those over sixty-five and over seventy-five, where the impact of aging is most pronounced and of principal concern. Data are provided on the number and proportions of older persons; sexual and racial composition of the older population; geographic variations for the number and proportion of elderly persons by states, size of place, and urban and rural residence mortality and survival rates; and social and economic characteristics such as education, marital status and living arrangements, and work status and income.

_____. DEMOGRAPHIC ASPECTS OF AGING AND OLDER POPULATIONS IN THE UNITED STATES. Current Population Reports, Special Studies Series P-23, No. 59. Washington, D.C.: 1976.

_____. SOCIAL AND ECONOMIC CHARACTERISTICS OF THE METROPOLITAN AND NON-METROPOLITAN POPULATION 1970 AND 1974. Current Population Reports, Special Studies Series P-23, No. 55. Washington, D.C.: 1975.

This report covers statistical data on urban, suburban, and rural characteristics. Mobility of populations, educational patterns, and family structure are given detailed breakdowns. Population mobility patterns are provided through twenty tables in addition to statistical analysis.

_____. SOCIAL AND ECONOMIC CHARACTERISTICS OF THE OLDER POPULATION 1974. Current Population Reports, Special Studies Series P-23, No. 57. Washington, D.C.: 1974.

The statistics available in this report cover education, vocational training, and literacy in addition to specific demographic and economic data. Projections on population characteristics and size are made to the year 2000.

_____. THE SOCIAL AND ECONOMIC STATUS OF THE BLACK POPULATION IN THE UNITED STATES. Current Population Reports, Special Studies Series P-23, No. 54. Washington, D.C.: 1974.

Statistical data in this report cover the following areas: population growth, population composition and distribution, population income, labor force and business ownership, education, family, health, housing, voting patterns, and crime. Appendixes are included.

_____. A STATISTICAL PORTRAIT OF WOMEN IN THE CURRENT POPULATION REPORTS. Special Studies Series P-23, No. 58. Washington, D.C.: 1976.

Changing Population Patterns

This report details education, employment, and other characteristics of women in the United States. The contents are intended to provide a measure for progress toward social equality through the provision of various standards on which to judge future progress.

Section B

IMPROVEMENT OF INSTRUCTION
IN THE URBAN SCHOOL

Abram, Robert E., et al. EVALUATION OF EDUCATION OF INNER CITY
HANDICAPPED CHILDREN: CASE STUDIES IN FIVE CITIES. Vol. 1: FINAL
REPORT. Columbus, Ohio: Battelle Memorial Institute, Columbus Laborato-
ries, 1973. (ED 088 265)

> This report is an evaluation of the education of inner-city handi-
> capped children in five cities. It assesses present education pro-
> grams, making a comparison of services provided inner-city children
> with services provided noninner-city children, and determines the
> needs unique to handicapped children in inner-city areas. It also
> formulates alternative solutions for meeting educational needs, and
> develops recommendations pertinent to planning for resource utili-
> zation.

ALL DAY KINDERGARTEN. ESEA TITLE I, EARLY CHILDHOOD EDUCATION.
Cincinnati: Cincinnati Public Schools, 1974. (ED 108 143)

> This is a full-day session kindergarten serving disadvantaged, inner-
> city preschool children who score at or below the twenty-fifth per-
> centile on a preschool inventory. Activities are designed to in-
> crease motor, perceptual, and auditory skills, and language and
> concept development.

Allen, Hope E. "Fantasy or Reality? Education in the Inner City." CLEAR-
ING HOUSE 44 (February 1970): 356-59.

> The disadvantaged who live in the ghettos of American cities must
> be educated to face reality. This is the best preparation for them
> if they are to find a place for themselves in American society.

Anderson, James J., et al. MEXICAN-AMERICAN STUDENTS IN A METRO-
POLITAN CONTEXT: FACTORS AFFECTING THE SOCIAL-EMOTIONAL CLI-
MATE OF THE CLASSROOM. University Park: New Mexico State University,
1969. (ED 030 521)

> The study systematically explores social mechanisms of the class-
> room that mediate educational effects for Mexican Americans in a

metropolitan context. The study used seventy-two teachers from nine schools in three districts in El Paso, Texas. The identification of teacher-dominated classrooms related to affective relations with students, directness in classrooms, and the amount of empathy for Spanish-speaking students. The findings indicated two factors which affect teacher-student relationships--professional training of the teacher and the particular characteristics of the student body.

ANNUAL EVALUATION REPORT, 1970-71. EARLY CHILDHOOD EDUCATION LEARNING SYSTEM, FORT WORTH CENTRAL CITIES PROJECT. Austin, Tex.: Southwest Educational Development Laboratory, 1971. (ED 063 436)

This evaluation report, the third year of a project to give structural preschool experiences for children (ages two to five) from an econom-ically-deprived area of Fort Worth, contains a description of the program, program objectives, evaluation design, comparison groups, hypotheses to be tested, and results of the evaluation.

Arnez, Nancy L. "Preface: Urban Education, Calculated Design for Human Waste." JOURNAL OF NEGRO EDUCATION 44 (Summer 1975): 230-32.

The problem of large populations in inner-city schools is that the curriculum and methodology are built on a monolingual, mono-cultural, and norm-referenced graded framework which emphasizes the use of words while excluding the other symbol systems. This poor foundation is only confounded by the inadequate funds for schools, the lack of support for black administrators in large urban school districts, and the complex issue of segregation versus integra-tion. These issues are currently being viewed by black administra-tors in hopes of finding a solution.

Arnoff, Melvin. PROJECT FICSS (FOCUS ON INNER CITY SOCIAL STUDIES). FINAL REPORT. Youngstown, Ohio: Youngstown Board of Education, 1971. (ED 070 693)

The major objective of this project was to develop a new social studies curriculum for the inner city. Specific needs were to be addressed in developing the new social studies; the need for the curriculum to be an agent for developing the intellectual skills necessary for citizens to assimilate and process information so that they can better aid in determining policy, and the need to have a cohesive curriculum which is designed for the primary through the secondary grades.

Arthur, Rita. "The Community as Classroom: Three Experiments. The Butler Program of Education." NASSP BULLETIN 55 (May 1971): 153-58.

Barnes, Jarvis. PROFILES OF EFFECTIVENESS AND ACCEPTABILITY OF READ-ING AND ARITHMETIC PROGRAMS, 1971-72. Research and Development Re-port, vol. 6, no. 18, March 1973. Atlanta: Atlanta Public Schools, 1973. (ED 078 121)

This model can be used to identify the relative effectiveness and acceptability of pupil performance in grades two through seven in the Atlanta public school system. The report covers pupil performance during the 1971-72 school year. Reading and arithmetic are the two programs incorporated in the profiles.

Barrett, Donald N., and Samora, Julian. THE MOVEMENT OF SPANISH YOUTH FROM RURAL TO URBAN SETTINGS. Washington, D.C.: National Committee for Children and Youth, 1963. (ED 002 539)

This report deals with the problems faced by persons with Spanish surnames who move to the cities, and gives recommendations for improving their situation.

Bessent, Hattie, and Cage, B. N. PHASE II ASSESSMENT: RICHMOND VIRGINIA CAREER OPPORTUNITIES PROGRAM. Richmond: Richmond Public Schools, 1973. (ED 085 355)

The Career Opportunities Program (COP) in Richmond, which trained teachers from disadvantaged areas to return to the classrooms in those areas, was assessed. Fifty COP aides and fifty control students were administered opinionnaires, semantic differentials, the "How I See Myself Self-Concept Scale," and the "Myers-Briggs Type Indicator."

BETTER TOMORROW FOR THE URBAN CHILD. Flint, Mich.: Flint Board of Education, 1964. (ED 002 394)

This project was designed to help the inner-city child become a more effective citizen, both educationally and socially, through the use of additional human and material resources, and a realistic curriculum. The program focused on raising and improving student self-image and performance.

Bouchard, Ruth Ann, and Mackler, Bernard. THE UNFOLDING OF A PRE-KINDERGARTEN PROGRAM FOR FOUR YEAR OLDS. New York: Center for Urban Education, 1966. (ED 093 504)

This is an in-depth description of an early (1965) Headstart classroom for four-year-olds in Harlem, New York. It is based on direct, in-class observation, but standardized tests and interviews were also used. Teacher roles and behavior, curriculum, classroom behavior of the children, and parent-teacher and parent-school relationships are all discussed.

Braverman, Miriam. "Favorite Books of the Disadvantaged Youth." N.E.A. JOURNAL 55 (December 1966): 48-49.

Economically disadvantaged does not mean slow. The student may be slow because he has not mastered reading techniques, but he can be motivated to read. This article includes a list of books that range from DENNIS THE MENACE to THE INVISIBLE MAN, indicating the diversity of teenage interests.

Bremer, John. "ABC's of City Learning." SATURDAY REVIEW 55 (19 August 1972): 34-38.

> Bremer discusses the YELLOW PAGES OF LEARNING RESOURCES (M.I.T. Press), a catalog by the Group for Environmental Education showing how to use the city as a classroom.

Brummit, Huston, and Schieren, Anne G. "After the Perfect Set Up." PSYCHOLOGY IN THE SCHOOLS 11 (1974): 229-38.

> This article describes an intensive mental health program in a public elementary school in Brooklyn, New York. It discusses events and circumstances which hampered "the perfect set up."

Brunner, Jean. "Follow-Up on Follow-Through." GRADE TEACHER 89 (October 1971): 56-60.

> An innovational educational program is analyzed.

Burgess, Evangeline. VALUES IN EARLY CHILDHOOD EDUCATION. 2d ed. Washington, D. C.: National Education Association, 1965. (ED 088 565)

> This report summarizes research evidence of the values of early childhood education with emphasis on nursery school education. Abstracts of selected studies and bibliography are also included.

Burnett, Calvin W. "Urban Education in Low-Income Areas: An Overview." CATHOLIC EDUCATION REVIEW 67 (November 1969): 105-22.

> The poor receive an education that is unrelated to their needs and background. Vocational training, educational technology, school integration, and structure of school systems are among the areas in which change would make education more worthwhile to the disadvantaged.

Busch, Phyllis S. THE URBAN ENVIRONMENT: A TEACHER'S GUIDE, GRADES K-3. New York: Ferguson Publishing Co., 1975.

> Sixty-three learning activities comprise this curriculum guide to conservation education designed for elementary students.

Bush, M. Reid. "Were They Motivated?" SCIENCE TEACHER 36 (February 1969): 51-52.

Bushnell, Don D. "Black Arts for Black Youth." SATURDAY REVIEW 53 (18 July 1970): 43-46.

Black youth who study their own culture and art history can form a better perception of where they stand in the world and will more easily find a suitable career.

Cahill, Robert J., and Foley, Joseph J. EVALUATION AND EVALUATIVE RESEARCH IN AN URBAN BILINGUAL PROGRAM. Dedham, Mass.: Heuristics, 1973.

This is a report of a highly localized evaluation of the second year of a bilingual program in a large eastern city.

Caplovitz, David. THE POOR PAY MORE. New York: Free Press, 1967.

Actual case studies were cited stating statistics of fraudulent advertising practices trying to get poor people to pay more for a product than its actual cost. Solution to the problem was directed at the schools improving consumer education, better understanding by poor people of themselves as consumers, adequate incomes, occupations, and reduced discrimination.

Chrein, George. "Agricultural Career Education in the City of New York." AGRICULTURAL EDUCATION MAGAZINE 47 (January 1975): 149-50, 152.

More than one thousand students in ten high schools throughout New York City are presently enrolled in an agricultural career program, specializing in farm production and management, ornamental horticulture, animal care, or conservation.

Clair, Joseph. "Urban Education and the Exceptional Child: A Legal Analysis." JOURNAL OF NEGRO EDUCATION 42 (Summer 1973): 351-59.

This article reviews cases which develop a legal definition of universal education, a concept which has provided the basis for placing students in special classes thereby providing special education. This development has resulted in the idea that all are entitled to an appropriate education and that school administrators must find ways to implement this humane concept. Making the assumption that this concept will be carried out, the author considers the possibility of having well-adjusted and educated normal and exceptional children.

Clark, Stephen C., et al. URBAN EDUCATION SYSTEMS ANALYSIS. Washington, D. C.: National Center for Educational Statistics, 1967. (ED 013 528)

Analysis of urban educational systems may be achieved by use of an analytical model. The model may be used in decision-making regarding school location, enrollment, facilities, organization, programs, and costs. Known data such as monies available, staff allocation, and current school plant are introduced into the model.

CLASSROOM PRACTICES IN TEACHING ENGLISH. 1969-1970. FOCUS: MINORITIES: COMMUNICATING THE DREAM'S RESPONSIBILITY. Champaign, Ill.: National Council of Teachers of English, 1969. (ED 076 997)

> This collection of articles focuses on Afro-American ideas, communication, and teaching in the megalopolis.

THE COGNITIVELY ORIENTED URBAN PREKINDERGARTEN. AN ESEA TITLE III SECOND YEAR REPORT. West Chester, Pa.: West Chester State College, 1974. (ED 104 536)

> This report gives a program description and evaluation of the second year of operation of this developmental educational program for low income black and Puerto Rican families. The program is designed to provide a link between the Early Learning Program of the Pennsylvania Research in Infant Development and Education Project (PRIDE) and kindergarten in the school system with the goal of preventing educational regression.

THE COGNITIVELY ORIENTED URBAN PREKINDERGARTEN: A TITLE III ESEA FIRST YEAR REPORT. West Chester, Pa.: West Chester Educational Development Center, 1973. (ED 091 060)

> To meet the needs of increasing numbers of disadvantaged children moving into the area, a cognitively oriented preschool was implemented in West Chester. Effects of the program were assessed in the following areas: parent and community acceptance, operational strengths and weaknesses, behavioral changes in participating children, and intellectual, language, and social growth in participating children.

Cohrs, Ray M., et al. DETROIT, MICHIGAN--A STUDY OF BARRIERS TO EQUAL EDUCATIONAL OPPORTUNITY IN A LARGE CITY. REPORT OF AN INVESTIGATION. Washington, D.C.: National Education Association, 1967. (ED 011 705)

> In March 1966, the Detroit Education Association requested that the National Commission on Professional Rights and Responsibilities of the National Education Association conduct a full scale investigation of the alleged gross inequality of educational opportunities available to Detroit's youth. The commission discovered that the root of the problem lay in the structure and substance of the urban society itself. The commission recommended development of the center city in the areas of (1) fiscal reform, (2) teacher preparation, (3) urban planning, (4) de facto segregation, (5) higher education, and (6) public relations.

Cook, Jennifer Margaret Mortimer. "Programmed Tutoring In Reading: A Study of the Use of Out-of-School Neighborhood Youth Corps Enrollees as Tutors to Low-Achieving Behaviorally Disordered Children in the Regular Classrooms of an Inner-City Elementary School." Ph.D. dissertation, University of Kentucky, 1973.

This study examines the effects of programmed tutoring in specified subjects for students who have been labeled behaviorally disordered. The study used experimental and control groups to measure significant differences over the fifty-day period. This yielded no significant differences in measures of performance achievement, but there was some improvement in the behavior of the experimental group.

Cooney, Joan Ganz. CHILDREN'S TELEVISION WORKSHOP. PROGRESS REPORT. New York: Children's Television Workshop, 1974. (ED 095 892)

Results of a nationwide research study indicate how many watch the program, "The Electric Company," at home and at school. Research indicates it is meeting its reading instruction objective. Only some changes in emphasis will be made. "Sesame Street's" new programming will treat more fully the bilingual-bicultural areas as well as the area of emotions.

Crenshaw, Joseph W., and Smith, Rodney P. "Urban Learning Environments, Opportunities, and Procedures." REVITALIZING EDUCATION IN THE BIG CITIES. Denver: Colorado State Department of Education, 1972. (ED 065 916)

This chapter suggests procedures and alternative practices for the improvement of big-city education. The authors (1) urge the importance of planning, (2) describe procedures for identifying and selecting promising alternative practices, (3) discuss the involvement of people in urban education, (4) identify emerging learning environments, (5) suggest ideas that offer alternatives to traditional schooling, and (6) outline strategies for improving education.

D'Amico, Donald J., and Janes, Edward V. "A Migrant Project in an Inner City." ILLINOIS SCHOOL JOURNAL 53 (Spring-Summer 1973): 25-29.

This article describes a federal program which attacked academic deficits of migrant children in Joliet, Illinois. Components of the project included instructional activities, development of materials, staff development, ancillary services, as well as parent and community involvement.

Davidoff, Stephen H. "The Crossroad of Urban Education--Title I ESEA." URBAN EDUCATION 9 (July 1974): 152-60.

Davidoff examines the Title I, ESEA projects in Philadelphia, and argues that those behind the overall federal effort have been confused about its purpose, evaluation criteria, and the relatively short span of time that has elapsed between its inception and the measurement of program impact.

Davidoff, Stephen H., et al. "Reading Skill Centers: A Comprehensive Attack on Reading Problems Commonly Encountered in Urban Schools." Paper presented at the meeting of the American Educational Research Association, New York, New York, 7 February 1971. (ED 047 892)

> Seven reading skill centers were established to focus on areas of need experienced by Philadelphia school children. Programs were individually prescribed, and children were assigned to materials and to center time depending on their individual needs. It was concluded (1) that reading performance, word attack skills, and comprehension skills were improved by the program, and (2) that the combination of diagnosis and individual prescription with provision for sufficient and individualized instruction appeared to be a fruitful approach toward reversing underachievement in urban schools.

Davis, Dick. "One Solution to the Inner-City Attendance Problem." PHI DELTA KAPPAN 56 (April 1975): 560.

> The author describes a process and a structure that reduced absenteeism in an inner-city school.

Davis, Richard H. "The Failures of Compensatory Education." EDUCATION AND URBAN SOCIETY 4 (February 1972): 234-48.

Demsch, Berthold, and Friedman, Lorraine. "The Use of Urban Community Resources to Expand School Social Work Service." JOURNAL OF THE INTERNATIONAL ASSOCIATION OF PUPIL PERSONNEL WORKERS 13 (March 1969): 80-86.

Densham, William E. "Vocational Agriculture Brightens Future of Big City Students." AGRICULTURAL EDUCATION MAGAZINE 47 (January 1975): 151-52.

> The program of the nation's only high school devoted strictly to agriculture-related programs is described. Paradoxically located in the nation's fourth-largest city (Philadelphia), it boasts the world's largest Future Farmers of America chapter.

DETROIT GREAT CITIES SCHOOL IMPROVEMENT PROJECT, ANNUAL REPORT, 1962-63. Detroit: Great Cities Program, 1963. (ED 001 050)

> Noting that the child of limited background has considerable native ability but has not been able to reach his potential due to the kind of teaching and curriculum offered in the typical public school, the Detroit project has attempted to compensate for the difficulties resulting from deprivation.

DIAGNOSTIC-PRESCRIPTIVE-INDIVIDUALIZED (DPI) PRIMARY READING PROGRAM. Louisville, Ky.: Louisville University, 1974. (ED 106 783)

> This program serves over thirty-one hundred first, second, and third grade predominantly disadvantaged children. Junior high school

students participate in the program as cross-age tutors. The emphasis is on reading and language development, with children working from educational prescriptions prepared at the beginning of each of ten three-week cycles.

DISTRICT NUMBER 22 STATE URBAN EDUCATION PROJECTS. New York: New York University, New York Center for Field Research and School Services, 1972. (ED 087 832)

Four projects are evaluated in this report: (1) The Diagnostic and Remedial Reading Center which provides intensive instruction in reading, (2) Teacher Training for New and Inexperienced Teachers Program, (3) The JHS Reading Laboratories Program (special reading program in junior high schools), and (4) The Educational Assistants to Aid Underachievers Program (early identification and remediation of first graders with reading problems).

Doll, Russell C., and Hawkins, Maxine, eds. EDUCATING THE DISADVANTAGED, 1970-1971. New York: A.M.S. Press, 1971.

The book is organized into five parts: (1) introductory perspectives on educating the disadvantaged, (2) who are the disadvantaged, (3) class, race, and society, (4) programs and prospects, and (5) metropolitanism and the ecosystem.

Dror, Yehezkel. URBAN METAPOLICY AND URBAN EDUCATION. Santa Monica, Calif.: RAND Corp., 1970. (ED 051 343)

The main thesis of this paper is that innovative changes in both urban metapolicy and in urban education are needed to meet present and future urban problems. Metapolicy deals with policies on policymaking, including the characteristics of the policymaking system and basic policy frameworks and postures.

Dunn, Lloyd M., and Mueller, Max W. DIFFERENTIAL EFFECTS ON THE I.T.P.A. ILLINOIS TEST OF PSYCHOLINGUISTIC ABILITIES PROFILE OF THE EXPERIMENTAL VERSION OF LEVEL #1 OF THE PEABODY LANGUAGE DEVELOPMENT KITS WITH DISADVANTAGED FIRST GRADE CHILDREN. Imrid Papers and Reports, vol. 4, no. 6. Nashville: George Peabody College for Teachers, Institute on Mental Retardation and Intellectual Development, 1967. (ED 105 447)

The experimental group (529) of first grade children received a daily thirty-minute oral language stimulation exercise from the Peabody Language Development Kit (PLDK) throughout the school year. This was contrasted with a control group of 203 children. The differential effects of the experimental revision of level of the PLDK on the ITPA (Illinois Test of Psycholinguistic Abilities) profiles of the disadvantaged first grade children were studied. The program was differentially effective, and these effects are reported.

_____. THE EFFICACY OF THE INITIAL TEACHING ALPHABET AND THE PEABODY LANGUAGE DEVELOPMENT KIT WITH GRADE ONE DISADVANTAGED CHILDREN: AFTER ONE YEAR. Imrid Papers and Reports, vol. 3, no. 2. Nashville: George Peabody College for Teachers, Institute on Mental Retardation and Intellectual Development, 1966. (ED 105 440)

> The efficacy of the ITA (Initial Teaching Alphabet) in teaching beginning reading and the PLDK in stimulating oral language and verbal intelligence of underpriviledged first grade children was studied. Pupil progress was measured in school achievement, language development, and intellectual growth.

Durhas, Paul, Jr. "Teaching Motor Skills to the Mentally Retarded." EXCEPTIONAL CHILDREN 35 (May 1969): 739-44.

> Various techniques in teaching motor skills are suggested and discussed to benefit the beginning teacher working with the mentally retarded.

EDEN GARDENS KINDERGARTEN PROGRAM. Shreveport, La.: Caddo Parrish School Board, 1974. (ED 106 835)

> This all-day kindergarten program serves sixty-one children, mostly disadvantaged blacks. It is the first phase in the district-wide continuous progress program in reading. The sequential stages in the development of reading skills are outlined and presented in behavioral objective form.

EDUCATION AND MANPOWER STRATEGIES AND PROGRAMS FOR DEPRIVED URBAN NEIGHBORHOODS: THE MODEL CITIES APPROACH. FINAL REPORT. Washington, D.C.: National League of Cities, 1968. (ED 025 629)

> This report attempts to identify effective strategies that might be used by city and school administrators in planning, initiating, and coordinating comprehensive deprived neighborhood manpower and education programs.

EDUCATION FOR THE URBAN DISADVANTAGED: FROM PRESCHOOL TO EMPLOYMENT. New York: New York Research and Policy Committee, 1971. (ED 050 189)

> This report of the Committee for Economic Development focuses on findings which indicate that while American schools have succeeded with middle and upper income youth, they have commonly failed with educating disadvantaged urban youths.

ESEA TITLE I, CHILD PARENT CENTERS, 1972-73. FINAL EVALUATION REPORT. Arlington, Va.: Institute for the Development of Educational Auditing, 1974. (ED 095 228)

These eleven centers are in areas with a high density of low-income families. Six years of education (ages three through nine) are offered. The purpose of the program is to build a strong foundation for cognitive and affective growth, with different techniques and approaches used to accomplish this.

Estes, Sidney H. "Instruction-Inner City: 'Where It's Really At.'" EDUCATIONAL LEADERSHIP 32 (March 1975): 384–87.

Teachers, programs, and facilities suitable to the special needs and potentials of inner-city youngsters must be provided.

AN EVALUATION: IMPROVEMENT OF TEACHING ENGLISH AS A SECOND LANGUAGE. New York: New York University, New York Center for Field Research and School Services, 1973. (ED 087 840)

The objective of this project was to improve the facility of English-language handicapped students in the four language skills (listening, speaking, reading, and writing) so they could make a proper adjustment to high school. The project involved as many as twenty different language groups, but most of the students were from Spanish-speaking or French-speaking backgrounds.

AN EVALUATION OF A PROGRAM OF READING ACCELERATION, REMEDIATION AND ENRICHMENT FOR SECONDARY SCHOOL STUDENTS IN POVERTY AREAS. NEW YORK STATE URBAN EDUCATION PROGRAM. FINAL REPORT. New York: New York University, New York Center for Field Research and School Services, 1972. (ED 087 833)

This program was designed for eleventh and twelfth grade students reading between a 4.0 and 7.0 grade equivalency range. The overall objective of the program was to improve reading comprehension ability and attitudes and to raise the level of reading proficiency to the 8.0 criterion necessary for diploma qualification in New York City.

AN EVALUATION OF ESEA TITLE I PROGRAMS, COMMUNITY SCHOOL DISTRICT 15. New York: New York University, Center for Field Research and School Services, 1973. (ED 087 842)

EVALUATION OF STATE URBAN EDUCATION PROGRAMS, DISTRICT 10, NEW YORK CITY, BOARD OF EDUCATION. 1970-1971 SCHOOL YEAR. Bronx, N.Y.: Fordham University, Institute for Research and Evaluation, 1971. (ED 059 017)

Seven New York City urban education programs were evaluated under the direction of the state urban education coordinator, and these are the evaluation reports. Each report consists of sections on program objectives, evaluation objectives and procedures, program implementation, program effectiveness, and recommendations. Tables are included.

AN EVALUATION OF THE BILINGUAL CENTER FOR PRESCHOOLERS IN DISTRICT 17, ESEA TITLE VII PROGRAM. New York: New York University, New York Center for Field Research and School Services, 1973. (ED 087 844)

> This report gives the objectives and major findings of a bilingual center for preschoolers in New York City. Some of the objectives are: improvement of communication skills in the first language, development of a comparable ability in a second language, development of parental concern and involvement in the program, and an increase in teacher awareness of the value of bilingualism.

AN EVALUATION OF THE CORRECTIVE MATHEMATICS SERVICES FOR DISADVANTAGED PUPILS IN NON-PUBLIC SCHOOLS. ESEA TITLE I PROGRAM. New York: New York University, New York Center for Field Research and School Services, 1972. (ED 087 835)

> This program was proposed to serve 14,032 poverty area children in 165 nonpublic regular day schools. Children eligible for the project had scores on a standardized test in mathematics more than one standard deviation below the grade norm. Licensed teachers provided the corrective services as an in-school program during regular school hours.

AN EVALUATION OF THE ESEA TITLE I AND STATE URBAN PROGRAMS: COMMUNITY SCHOOL DISTRICT, NEW YORK CITY BOARD OF EDUCATION. FINAL REPORT. New York: Teaching and Learning Research Corp., 1974. (ED 096 365)

> This document covers twelve Community School District 1 ESEA Title I programs and State Urban Education programs. The Comprehensive Reading Program had four components. The Bilingual-Bicultural Program was funded jointly by Title I and Title VII. The Elementary Bilingual Program afforded Spanish-speaking pupils an early opportunity to experience academic success. The Chinese-English Bilingual Program provided remedial support for Chinese children. The Secondary Bilingual Program provided instruction in major course areas in Spanish while teaching English as a second language.

AN EVALUATION OF THE READINESS PROGRAM FOR DISADVANTAGED PRE-SCHOOL CHILDREN WITH EXCEPTIONAL LEARNING DISABILITIES. New York: New York University, Center for Field Research of Education, 1973. (ED 087 839)

> The Readiness Program for Disadvantaged Pre-School Children with Exceptional Learning Disabilities, New York State's Urban Education Quality Incentive Program, provides educational, clinical, and

socialization services to children who manifest developmental problems in the areas of language functioning, social and emotional adjustment, fine and gross motor development, activity levels, and
cognitive development.

EVALUATION OF TITLE I DECENTRALIZED UMBRELLA AND TITLE I OPTIONAL
ASSIGNMENT PROGRAMS FOR DISADVANTAGED PUPILS. DISTRICT 24, NEW
YORK CITY. New York: New York University, New York Center for Field
Research and School Services, 1973. (ED 087 845)

This report deals with special educational services supplementing
the regular school programs (1972-73 school year) in this district.
The programs involved were: prekindergarten, early childhood, bilingual community liaison, trainable mentally retarded, nonpublic
school, English as a second language, corrective reading, and
guidance. Objectives are given in each program.

EVALUATION REPORT, DISTRICT 24, QUEENS. TITLE I DISTRICT UMBRELLA
AND TITLE I OPEN ENROLLMENT EDUCATIONAL SERVICES FOR DISADVAN-
TAGED PUPILS. New York: New York University, New York Center for
Field Research and School Services, 1972. (ED 087 829)

In the 1971-72 school year, supplemental educational services were
added to regular educational programs through funds received under
Title I ESEA. The programs funded are treated in this evaluation
report under the following headings: prekindergarten program,
strengthened early childhood program, corrective reading program,
bilingual community liaison, educational assistance for the mentally retarded, English as a second language, nonpublic schools
program, after-school study center, guidance services, and appendixes.

EVALUATIVE ASSESSMENT OF EXEMPLARY PRE-SERVICE TEACHER TRAINING
FOR INNER-CITY ELEMENTARY TEACHERS. Vol. 6: INNER-CITY TEACHING
STRATEGIES. Los Angeles: Contemporary Research, 1972. (ED 073 102)

This is a manual for teachers presenting the strategies and techniques
mentioned by inner-city teachers for handling prevalent problems.

EXECUTIVE ABSTRACTS: SUMMARY OF THE TITLE I EVALUATION, 1971-72
SCHOOL YEAR. Los Angeles: Los Angeles City Schools, Measurement and
Evaluation Branch, 1972. (ED 075 533)

Activities funded under Title I of the 1965 Elementary Secondary
Education Act evaluated in this report were in progress in eighty-
two elementary schools, fifteen junior and two senior high schools,
forty-five nonpublic schools, three schools for the handicapped,
and twenty-four special institutions during the 1971-72 school year
in Los Angeles.

Fahrer, Kimberly, and Vivolo, Robert, eds. DOCTORAL DISSERTATIONS ON URBAN AND MINORITY EDUCATION. New York: Columbia University, ERIC Clearinghouse on the Urban Disadvantaged, 1976.

> This volume contains two hundred and forty-five entries from January 1975 through May 1976.

Fesler, Elizabeth, et al. "Changes in Scholastic Achievement of Disadvantaged Children Enrolled in Follow-Through--PEP-IPI Project." Paper presented at the annual meeting of the American Educational Research Association, Washington, D.C., 30 March-3 April 1975. (ED 108 750)

> This paper summarizes the findings of a study of the effects of the Follow-Through Primary Education Project--Individually Prescribed Instruction (PEP-IPI) Model. This project was designed to provide individualized instruction to disadvantaged children (K-3d grade). Emphasis was placed on perceptual and motor abilities, language concepts, classifying skills, and reasoning abilities.

Flax, Michael J. A STUDY IN COMPARATIVE URBAN INDICATORS: CONDITIONS IN EIGHTEEN LARGE METROPOLITAN AREAS. Washington, D.C.: Urban Institute, 1972.

> The revised and expanded version is made of an initial Urban Institute research report on urban indicators. The original report presented indicators of fourteen quality-of-life categories for eighteen large metropolitan areas. This revision introduces new indicators for four of these categories and updates indicators for nine of the fourteen categories. The indicators are employed to develop charts and summary tables using the Washington, D.C. metropolitan area as an illustrative example.

Frankel, Max G.; Happ, F. William; and Smith, Maurice P. FUNCTIONAL TEACHING OF THE MENTALLY RETARDED. Springfield, Ill.: Charles C. Thomas, Publisher, 1966.

> This is a good basic text on teaching physical perceptual skills to the mentally handicapped. Well illustrated, the book includes resource material for practitioners.

Glassman, Alan M., and Belasco, James A. "Appealed Grievances in Urban Education." EDUCATION AND URBAN SOCIETY 7 (November 1974): 73-87.

> The study examines the nature and use of appealed grievances in an urban school district. The research reveals that actions taken by teacher organizations in pursuit of grievance resolutions are often more politically than organizationally beneficial. Neither school board nor teacher organization appeared to desire to find methods and tools to resolve conflict.

Gordon, Roger L. "Portrait of an Inner-City School." AUDIOVISUAL INSTRUCTION 16 (January 1971): 39-40.

Gordon describes a middle magnet school, that is a school which brings together teachers and students who have the most to gain from the nontraditional school climate.

Gowan, John Curtis. THE DISADVANTAGED AND POTENTIAL DROPOUT: COMPENSATORY EDUCATIONAL PROGRAMS. Springfield, Ill.: Charles C. Thomas, Publisher 1966.

This is a book of readings, but in addition, the author has placed in suitable chapters a considerable addition of annotated bibliographic references.

Gravzy, Rita. THE DALE AVENUE PROJECT: A PERFORMANCE OBJECTIVE CURRICULUM FOR PREKINDERGARTEN THROUGH THIRD GRADE. Final Project Report. Trenton, N.J.: State Department of Education, Office of Program Development; Paterson, N.J.: Board of Education, 1974. (ED 097 104)

This report describes a performance-objective curriculum designed to help disadvantaged prekindergarten and kindergarten urban children attain the skills required to be at grade level in reading and mathematics and at the national norm in I.Q. by grade one. It is designed to systematically develop students' skills in ten critical areas.

GREAT CITIES RESEARCH COUNCIL EDUCATIONAL COMMUNICATIONS PROJECT. FINAL REPORT. Chicago: Research Council of the Great Cities Program for School Improvement, 1969. (ED 031 871)

Surveys of the data processing systems and the innovations in instruction and resource materials in sixteen school districts in the cities of Baltimore, Boston, Buffalo, Chicago, Cleveland, Detroit, Los Angeles, Memphis, Milwaukee, New York, Philadelphia, Pittsburgh, San Diego, San Francisco, St. Louis, and Washington, D.C., are detailed in this report.

Griffith, Lynda W., et al. EVALUATION OF EARLY CHILDHOOD EDUCATION: A MODEL CITIES SUPPORTED PRESCHOOL PROGRAM. Kansas City, Mo.: Institute for Community Studies, 1971. (ED 103 473)

Questions developed as evaluation goals for Model Cities Agency's program for children in Model Cities neighborhoods are considered here. Each question is treated in succession with summaries provided after each section.

Haberman, Martin. "Materials for Disadvantaged Need--and Don't Need." EDUCATIONAL LEADERSHIP 24 (April 1967): 611-17.

The author identifies materials which have been developed from the assumption that adding to the children's language codes should be the major purpose of special programs.

Halliburton, Warren J. "Inner City Education--Studying the Studies." PER-
SPECTIVES IN EDUCATION 6 (Spring 1963): 14-19.

> Standing at the vantage point of the 1970s, the author looks back
> at some of the studies produced in the 1960s, calling education and
> educators to task for the failings of the teaching-learning process in
> the inner city.

HANDBOOK FOR LANGUAGE ARTS: PRE-KINDERGARTEN, KINDERGARTEN,
GRADES ONE AND TWO. Curriculum Bulletin, 1965-66 Series No. 8. Brooklyn:
New York City Board of Education, 1966. (ED 021 859)

> This handbook, for prekindergarten through grade two, is one of a
> series of five language-arts guides being developed. Materials are
> specified in listening, speaking, writing, reading, and literature.
> It is aimed at urban children and suggests ways of adapting instruc-
> tion and materials.

Harrington, Fred W.; Thompson, John L.; and Koning, Hendrik B. "Making
Education Relevant in the Inner City." AMERICAN VOCATIONAL JOURNAL
47 (May 1972): 30-31.

> The Academy of Applied Electrical Science is described as the "pro-
> totype of a series of high school academies which represent an at-
> tempt to make public school education more relevant to the inner
> city environment." Actually, it is a new kind of school located
> in an underprivileged area at Thomas Edison High School in Phila-
> delphia which involves business and industry in vocational training
> in the electrical and electronic fields. It is aimed specifically at
> youth who are not college bound and who might otherwise become
> dropouts. The authors feel that the academy is a model which
> is a "tonic for the prevailing apathy towards the educational
> process" and can serve as an eye-opener in the future for voca-
> tional education.

HARTFORD MOVES AHEAD: AN EVALUATIVE REPORT. HEADSTART CHILD
DEVELOPMENT 1973-74. Hartford, Conn.: Hartford Public Schools, 1974.
(ED 105 972)

> This report discusses the gains in academic achievement and social
> development of 248 preschool children as measured by standardized
> tests, parent questionnaires, and staff surveys.

Havighurst, Robert J. "Curriculum for the Disadvantaged." PHI DELTA
KAPPAN 51 (March 1970): 371-73.

> This paper presents recommendations for the education of the chil-
> dren of the poorest 20 percent of the American population in the
> 1970s: (1) preschool programs for improving cognitive and language
> development, (2) elementary teachers who have learned more ways
> to reward for achievement, (3) orderly classrooms, where pupils

know that they will be rewarded for today's effort, and (4) relatively small adaption in curriculum to fit specific deficiencies and self-image needs of children and youth.

Hawke, Sharryl. THE SCHOOL OF URBAN STUDIES: A SCHOOL WITHIN A SCHOOL. PROFILES OF PROMISE 34. Boulder, Colo.: Social Science Education Consortium, 1974. (ED 100 732)

A student program to combat chronic absenteeism, suspension, and behavior problems was implemented in September 1972, at Memorial Junior High School in San Diego. The major aim of the program was to develop a small school environment to foster the growth of the whole student.

Heidenreich, Richard R., ed. URBAN EDUCATION. Arlington, Va.: College Readings, 1971.

URBAN EDUCATION is a collection of readings grouped into eight chapters covering the following topics: compensatory education, curriculum, decentralization, disadvantaged children, black positions, the ghetto, teachers and administrators, and big city problems. All material is current between 1968 and 1971. The only areas not considered are that of court decisions, financing urban education, unionism, accountability, and alternative schools.

Hellmuth, Jerome, ed. DISADVANTAGED CHILD. Vol. 3: COMPENSATORY EDUCATION: A NATIONAL DEBATE. New York: Brunner/Mazel Publishers, 1970. (ED 044 470)

Many papers on all aspects of the compensatory education debate are presented in this volume. Part 1 gives an overall picture. Part 2 deals with culture--fair testing, "Jensenism" and intelligence, and the significance of I.Q. testing with the study of racial differences. Part 3 is about problems of educating inner-city children and populations with differential characteristics, modification of cognitive skills, instructional techniques, and major programs geared to the needs of disadvantaged children.

HIGH HORIZONS 100, 1973-74. HARTFORD MOVES AHEAD: AN EVALUATIVE REPORT. Hartford, Conn.: Hartford Public Schools, 1974. (ED 098 267)

This is a report of a program conceived as a nineth grade center where a compensatory program would be offered.

Hood, Elizabeth F. EDUCATING BLACK STUDENTS: SOME BASIC ISSUES. Detroit: Detroit Educational Consultants, 1973. (ED 084 327)

This collection contains the following articles: (1) "Education: Opening the Survival Kit," (2) "Delusion of Progress: Education in the Public Schools, " (3) "The Impossible Dream," (4) "Language and Learning," (5) "A Look Inside--The C School, The P School, The R School," (6) "The Made People Versus the Creative People: A Dilemma in Urban Education As Seen by a Black Administrator," (7) "What Should be Taught to Black Children?," (8) "Education is Learning Together," (9) "Leadership in Black Students," (10) "It Has Been Done," and (11) "The Black Experience: Implications for New Dimensions in Education."

Houts, Paul L. "Generation in the Wind." NATIONAL ELEMENTARY PRIN-CIPLE 48 (May 1969): 98-107.

Howe, Harold II. "The Frustrations of Progress." Paper presented before the annual conference of the American Association of School Administrators, Atlantic City, New Jersey, 1968. (ED 020 976)

> Six recommendations given for a progressive agenda in education which demand attention from every school are: (1) renewed emphasis on preschool education, (2) concentrated attention on reducing the isolation of the schools, (3) coordinated work-study programs for junior and senior high school students, (4) preservice and inservice training with emphasis on special programs for inner-city schools, (5) increased emphasis on individualized instruction and self-directed learning, and (6) new efforts designed to achieve racial integration.

Howell, Barbara Thompson. PARTNERS IN URBAN EDUCATION: GETTING IT TOGETHER AT HOME. Morristown, N.J.: General Learning Corporation, 1972. (ED 104 993)

> This handbook is written for the parents of school-age children and provides suggestions for working with the child, teachers, other parents, and ways of using the home and community to help the child learn.

Hunnicutt, C. W. URBAN EDUCATION AND CULTURAL DEPRIVATION. Syracuse, N. Y.: Syracuse University, 1964. (ED 001 435)

> Aspects of programs for the culturally deprived are discussed in the areas of (1) support, (2) home and neighbors, (3) the student, and (4) the school. Specific problems are identified such as financing programs which are caused by unequal tax bases in the cities, the apparent unconcern of the states for the cities, and the unfeasibility of the federal government becoming involved with every major city in the nation in order to equalize opportunities.

Hunt, Barbara C., et al. "Teaching Reading in an Inner City School: A Program That Works." READING TEACHER 27 (October 1973): 25-28.

> This essay presents the results of a Title I program serving severely deprived children who have been identified as having reading difficulties.

Hunt, J. McVicker, ed. HUMAN INTELLIGENCE. New Brunswick, N.J.: Transaction Books, 1972.

INTENSIVE READING INSTRUCTIONAL TEAMS (IRIT), 1971-1972. Hartford, Conn.: Hartford Public Schools, 1972. (ED 066 707)

> Intensive compensatory reading instruction was provided for more than five hundred Hartford third, fourth, and fifth grade students in the 1971-72 school year. The approach was geared to the concept of individualized learning and instruction, student self-direction, and program accountability.

INTENSIVE SERVICES FOR EARLY CHILDHOOD AND ELEMENTARY SCHOOL AGE DISADVANTAGED STUDENTS: EVALUATION OF THE ESEA TITLE I COMPENSATORY EDUCATION PROGRAM OF THE SAN FRANCISCO UNIFIED SCHOOL DISTRICT, 1969-1970. A REPORT. San Francisco: San Francisco Unified School District, 1971. (ED 049 331)

> This program involved schools in need of intensified educational services for a population of disadvantaged students. Integral components of the program included language development, mathematics, inservice education, auxiliary services, parental involvement, and intergroup experiences.

Israel, Benjamin L. RESPONSIVE ENVIRONMENT PROGRAM: BROOKLYN, NEW YORK: REPORT OF THE FIRST FULL YEAR OF OPERATION. THE TALKING TYPEWRITER. Brooklyn: New York City Board of Education, 1968. (ED 027 742)

> This is a report of a research and demonstration project for disadvantaged students using the talking typewriter.

Jamison, Sandra, and Campbell, Bruce. POLLUTION: PROBLEMS AND SOLUTIONS. Youngstown, Ohio: Youngstown Board of Education, 1971. (ED 104 794)

> This is the first unit of a ninth grade section dealing with ecological crises involving pollution and its causes. Specific teaching procedures are outlined to aid the teacher in developing the concepts of the unit.

Janowitz, Morris. INSTITUTION BUILDING IN URBAN EDUCATION. Chicago: University of Chicago Press, 1971.

> This book addresses itself to the problem of changing the slum school. Janowitz begins by noting that progress made in this area over the past twenty years is insignificant. The two major crises that are identified are the persistence of gross inequities in educational resources, and the need to replace work organizations as a primary site for socialization. The economic constructs of today result in delayed access to the labor market which has lead to an

increasing demand for individuals to acquire a high school diploma.
This phenomenon has caused increased demands on inner-city schools,
but the necessary innovations and resources are not available to
meet these demands.

Jensen, Henry C. "A Time for Boldness--East San Jose Says 'Yes' to Educational Park Concept." JOURNAL OF SECONDARY EDUCATION 44 (January
1969): 31-35.

Johnson, Doris J., and Myklabust, Holmer R. LEARNING DISABILITIES: EDU-
CATIONAL PRINCIPLES AND PRACTICES. New York: Grune and Stratton,
1967.

> This book fills a need as a textbook for courses aimed at training
> teachers concerned with the intriguing problem of learning disabil-
> ities.

Johnson, James A., Jr., ed. ON THE INTERFACE BETWEEN LOW-INCOME,
URBAN BLACK CHILDREN AND THEIR TEACHERS DURING THE EARLY SCHOOL
YEARS: A POSITION PAPER. San Francisco: Far West Laboratory for Educa-
tional Research and Development, 1973. (ED 091 469)

> This position paper was initiated by Division IV (home-school linkage).
> The goals of the paper were: (1) to expose the reader to the as-
> sessment of educational research in the problem area, (2) to help
> to clarify a set of complex problems associated with interactions
> of low-income, urban black children and their teachers, and (3)
> to identify research areas in which more research is needed. An
> immediate purpose was to provide a base for the purpose of identi-
> fying a target area for further research and study.

Jones, Wendel P. RELEVANCE AND QUALITY OF EDUCATION FOR MINOR-
ITIES: PROJECT DESIGN. EDUCATIONAL NEEDS, FRESNO, 1968, NUMBER
26. Fresno, Calif.: Fresno City Unified School District, 1968. (ED 038 764)

> The general improvement of educational relevance and quality for
> minority groups in the Fresno City Unified School District is con-
> sidered as part of PROJECT DESIGN, funded under ESEA Title III.
> Selected schools were visited and conferences held with students,
> teachers, administrators, citizens, and black community leaders and
> parents. The recommendation accorded the highest priority is that
> educational developments, proposals, and achievements be communi-
> cated to the citizenry in general and to its minority population in
> particular.

Kelly, Eleanor A., and Turner, Deanna N. "Clothing Awareness and Feelings
of Deprivation and Satisfaction Among Lower Social Class First Grade Children."
JOURNAL OF HOME ECONOMICS 6 (June 1970): 396-400.

Because studies are limited, the purpose of this research was to develop and test an instrument to study the clothing awareness behavior of lower social class, preschool children. Barriers of verbal ability, motivation, and attention span of children had to be overcome in designing such an instrument for testing. The outcome was successful and indicates the attitudes of very young children are researchable when verbal ability and a manipulative feature are combined.

Kenefick, Barbara, and Paznik, Jane. THE LARC (LANGUAGE ACQUISITION RESOURCE CENTER) PROGRAM. New York: Center for Urban Education, 1970. (ED 089 339)

The purpose of the LARC project is to implement a home-based program which will help six-month to five-year-old children develop communication skills. It was set up as a pilot program for children of inner city or ghetto backgrounds, but the program is designed for children of all socioeconomic groups.

Koch, Edward Leo. "The Neighborhood School: The Relation of Social Area Factors and Residential Stability to Aggregate Pupil Achievement." Ed.D. dissertation, Cornell University, 1966.

This study considers the factors of social rank, ethnicity, urbanism, and residential stability as predictors of achievement in a medium size public school system. The relationships found in this selected study are explained and described in depth. The study would have to be replicated for generalization to other school systems.

Kolstoe, Oliver P. TEACHING EDUCABLE MENTALLY RETARDED CHILDREN. New York: Holt, Rinehart and Winston, 1970.

This is the latest book on the planning of educational programs for the EMH (educable mentally handicapped). It divides them into five levels of learning and carries each through.

Kruszynski, Eugene. "The Nature of Urban Education." SCHOOL AND SOCIETY 98 (March 1970): 166-68.

The purpose of urban education is to instruct the young in a way that will enable them to cope with their environment when they leave school.

Landes, Sandra R. ABBREVIATED VERSION OF THE 1971-72 FINAL EVALUATION REPORT PRESCHOOL FOR URBAN CHILDREN PROJECT. Princeton, N.J.: Educational Testing Service, 1972. (ED 071 748)

The two purposes of this project are: (1) to provide preschool education based on "Sesame Street" viewing, and (2) to provide an experimental framework to evaluate three possible approaches of parental involvement which might further help children viewing the program. The participants in the project were parent-child pairs. This is a report on the first operational year of the Preschool for Urban Children Project.

Landrum, John William. "The Effects of the Los Angeles County Neighborhood Youth Corps Program on the Performance of Enrollees in School." Ed.D. dissertation, University of Southern California, 1967.

Performance evaluation of enrollees in a Los Angeles County Neighborhood Youth Corps Work Training Project and the identification of project values were the focuses of this study. The performance measures indicated minimal but significant improvement in attendance and other behavior indicators. However, the author indicates that long-term impact of the program is questionable.

Lauchner, Jan. AN INSTRUCTIONAL PROGRAM DESIGNED FOR CHILDREN FROM BIRTH THROUGH SEVENTH GRADE: ED. S. COOK ELEMENTARY SCHOOL, 1972-73. Research and Development Report, vol. 7, no. 16, October 1973. Atlanta: Atlanta Public Schools, 1973. (ED 088 965)

The Ed. S. Cook Elementary School, located in Atlanta's inner city, served 666 pupils in grades kindergarten through seven in the main building and an additional 80 younger children in the Title IV, a child development center located in adjacent buildings. Supplementing the instructional program were three supportive programs.

Lawson, James H., and McClernon, Francis M. SUMMARY OF THE COOPERATIVE URBAN TEACHER EDUCATION EVALUATION, vol. 2, no. 1. Kansas City, Mo.: Mid Continent Regional Education Laboratory, 1969. (ED 043 600)

This is the second in a series of evaluation reports on the Cooperative Urban Teachers Education Program. After analysis of the evaluation data, fifteen recommendations were made for the improvement of the program. Included were interstaff idea exchange, better understanding of testing techniques, conferences for students, greater involvement of cooperating teachers, and opportunities for discussion of inner-city problems.

Leeper, Robert R., ed. CURRICULUM DECISIONS: SOCIAL REALITIES. Washington, D. C.: Association for Supervision and Curriculum Development, 1968. (ED 049 081)

This booklet reports six major presentations about the social forces that are molding or blasting the schools. In particular, Muriel Crosby discusses the developing problems of the city, its people, and its schools, along with some community and educational solutions to these problems. They included: redistricting, emphasis on quality education, inner-city teacher education programs, new strategies in teaching, curriculum building, and supervision.

Lessinger, Leon M. "Implications of Competency-Based Education for Urban Children." EDUCATIONAL TECHNOLOGY 12 (November 1972): 58-61.

> The author argues from three basic assumptions: (1) mastery of subject matter is the essence of education, (2) competition through formal systems ensures only that the intelligent and dedicated reach the top, and (3) ability of people is distributed along the normal curve. These assumptions in our present system have negatively affected the urban educational delivery system. The revival of the competency notion which emphasizes aptitude and the developmental characteristics is offered as an alternative to traditional approaches. The competency-based education system is contrasted with national needs with reference to the urban dilemma.

Levine, Daniel U. INNER CITY DISADVANTAGED AND THE METROPOLITAN BIND. Kansas City, Mo.: University of Missouri-Kansas City, Center for the Study of Metropolitan Problems in Education, 1971. (ED 057 127)

> This essay approaches the problem of education for the urban poor. The way in which the problems of large cities relate to the educational experience of disadvantaged children is discussed. The interrelated development of middle-class suburbs, blue-collar neighborhoods, and the central city are analyzed.

Lewis, Michael. "Weave Music into the Fabric of City Life." MUSIC EDUCATION JOURNAL 56 (April 1970): 64-66.

> An innovative program is presented here for teaching music in urban areas.

Lichten, William. DEVELOPMENT OF NEW INSTRUCTIONAL USES OF THE COMPUTER IN AN INNER-CITY COMPREHENSIVE HIGH SCHOOL. FINAL REPORT. New Haven, Conn.: Yale University, 1971. (ED 057 597)

> This report covers a three-part program investigating the use of computers at an inner-city high school. The parts of the program included: (1) an attempt to introduce a digital computer for instructional purposes at the high school, (2) an attempt to teach the FORTRAN programming language to a select group of gifted New Haven public high school pupils, and (3) an investigation of methods of training teachers to use computers as a tool of instruction.

Liddle, Gordon P., and Rockwell, Robert E. EDUCATION IMPROVEMENT FOR THE DISADVANTAGED IN AN ELEMENTARY SETTING. Springfield, Ill.: Charles C. Thomas, Publisher, 1967.

> This is a report on the work and experiences of a group of educators looking into educational improvements for the disadvantaged child.

Longo, Paul, et al. COMMUNITY SCHOOL DISTRICT NUMBER 1: AN EVAL-
UATION OF THE 1972-1973 STATE URBAN EDUCATION PROGRAMS. FINAL
REPORT. New York: Teaching and Learning Research Corp., 1973. (ED 094
057)

> This report discusses several programs in New York. Some of them
> were as follows: (1) the Uplifting Skills Program which attempted
> to improve the reading achievement of pupils through diagnosis and
> remediation of perceptual problems, and the creation of reading
> centers, (2) the Supportive Training for Inexperienced and New
> Teachers, and (3) the Mathematics Laboratory Project to identify
> third, fourth, and fifth grade children who were low achievers in
> mathematics.

Lutsky, Judi, comp. HEAD START AND FOLLOW THROUGH. 1972-1974:
AN ERIC ABSTRACT BIBLIOGRAPHY. Urbana, Ill.: ERIC Clearinghouse on
Early Childhood Education, 1974. (ED 097 131)

> Recent ERIC documents (123) about Project Head Start and Project
> Follow Through are cited in this selective bibliography with ab-
> stracts. Reports of research and evaluation, and program descrip-
> tions are included. Entries were taken from CIJE (Current Index
> to Journals in Education) and RESEARCH IN EDUCATION, January
> 1972 through August 1974.

MacCracken, Alan L., Jr. "Curriculum Reform for the Impoverished." AMERI-
CAN SECONDARY EDUCATION 1 (June 1971): 31-35.

> The author examines the problem of urban education and the im-
> plications for educators and disadvantaged youth, focusing on cur-
> riculum and background relevant to curriculum innovation.

MacDonald, W. Scott. BATTLE IN THE CLASSROOM: INNOVATIONS IN
CLASSROOM TECHNIQUES. Scranton, Pa.: Intext Educational Publishing,
1971.

> This book is written for the classroom teacher. It is concerned
> with identifying classroom processes and teaching styles. Documen-
> tation is available for the demonstration of deteriorating effects of
> teaching styles under certain conditions. The emphasis is on the
> environment and relating it to classroom events, to promote posi-
> tive learning outcomes.

McKelvey, Troy V., and Swanson, Austin D., eds. URBAN SCHOOL ADMIN-
ISTRATION. Beverly Hills, Calif.: Sage Publications, 1969.

> This document contains twelve papers presented at an institute for
> urban school administrators designed to deal with the contemporary
> urban educational problems incident to school educational oppor-
> tunity.

Maras, Lorene Ruth. "Evaluation of a Large City Remedial Reading Program." Ed.D. dissertation, Illinois State University, 1974.

This study sought to determine the effectiveness of a remedial reading program conducted in a large-city school district over a five-year span of time.

Marburger, Carl L. AN OVERVIEW OF TYPES OF GREAT CITIES SCHOOL IMPROVEMENT PROGRAMS. Detroit: Great Cities Program, 1963. (ED 001 037)

Because millions of Americans have been deprived of equal educational opportunities, cities of today realize their obligation to educate the culturally deprived. Culturally deprived children reflect indifference to responsibility, nonpurposeful activity, poor health habits, inadequate communication skills, little mastery of reading skills, and a sense of failure.

Marburger, Carl L., and Rasschaert, William M. A PLAN FOR EVALUATING MAJOR ACTIVITIES IN GREAT CITIES SCHOOL IMPROVEMENT PROGRAM. Detroit: Great Cities Program, 1962. (ED 001 002)

The guide is intended to assist project directors in their efforts to develop more systematic and thorough evaluation designs for the Great Cities School Improvement Program. Major dimensions of teaching-learning, school-community, and pupil-parent-teacher activities are listed.

Marland, Sidney P. PROBLEMS AND PROSPECTS OF EDUCATION IN THE BIG CITIES AS EXEMPLIFIED BY PITTSBURGH, PENNSYLVANIA. Urbana, Ill.: ERIC Clearinghouse on Early Childhood Education, 1968. (ED 022 542)

Racial integration and compensatory education are needed to solve the problems in the big cities. Compensatory programs, such as team teaching, transition rooms, preprimary education (including parental preprimary counseling), and expectant mothers' programs, can provide aid to those who need the extra help.

Martin, Charles. "Editorial Comment: Continuing Crisis of Urban Education." JOURNAL OF NEGRO EDUCATION 44 (Summer 1975): 225-29.

This article reviews the current theories on the urban student. The classifications of "dull," "slow," and "nonverbal" as applied to urban students are considered. The explanations of Frank Riessman, Bernard Mackley, and Mosely Giddings indicate that present theories of urban learning patterns are misleading.

Martinek, Sharon S. "Revolutionary Education: Reason and Ways." Paper presented at the American Sociological Association, New Orleans, Louisiana, 28 August 1972. (ED 071 199)

This paper defines revolutionary education as a qualitative change in the structure of educational institutions, and the ideology surrounding the functions and goals of those institutions.

A MASTER PLAN FOR OCCUPATIONAL EDUCATION IN METROPOLITAN DENVER. POSITION PAPER. Denver: Metropolitan State College, 1968. (ED 025 628)

In presenting a complete program of occupational education for the Denver metropolitan area, this proposal offers twelve criteria for consideration in conjunction with a particular occupational need.

Matzner, Seymour. "Teacher Bias in Pupil Evaluation: A Critical Analysis." JOURNAL OF TEACHER EDUCATION 22 (Spring 1971): 40-43.

Matzner feels, in view of teacher biases, that the teacher's role in evaluation should be for only the students' social and emotional growth, and all academic areas should be evaluated by means of standardized tests.

May, Florence A., and Guise, Gloria. INCREASING COMPATIBILITY BETWEEN EDUCATIONAL PRACTICES AND EDUCATIONAL NEEDS OF PUPILS WHO ARE BLACK. San Francisco: San Francisco Unified School District, 1972. (ED 085 448)

This document is divided into five parts. The first part, the preface, discusses anxiety felt by teachers who, for the first time, are trying to teach people whose culture and background they know little about. The second part includes brief summaries of the presentations made by the consultant. The third part is "Multi-cultural Education," and the fourth is "Implications of Blackness for the Junior High and Senior High School Teacher." A discussion of some educational resources available to the teacher is discussed. The fifth part consists of a compendium of reviews of five books in part or in whole discussing relevant studies.

Mecklenburgèr, James A. "The Performance Contract in Gary." PHI DELTA KAPPAN 52 (March 1971): 406-10.

Meeker, Robert J., and Weiler, Daniel W. "Education and Urban Society." EDUCATION AND URBAN SOCIETY 3 (February 1971): 129-43.

The author considers the premise that the present public education system is designed to meet the needs of the middle class and the affluent. The design of programs featured, such as structured and open-ended curriculum, education criteria, testing, and the ability of schools to direct students vocationally are surveyed. The author reviews in depth the design of education and its potential impact on societal interests.

Meissner, Judith A., et al. DISADVANTAGED CHILDREN AND THEIR FIRST
SCHOOL EXPERIENCES--ETS--HEAD START LONGITUDINAL STUDY: PRE-
SCHOOL TEACHERS OF DISADVANTAGED CHILDREN: CHARACTERISTICS
AND ATTITUDES. Princeton, N.J.: Educational Testing Service, 1973.
(ED 109 136)

> This study developed and used a questionnaire to collect data on
> Head Start and other preschool teachers who were teaching longitu-
> dinal study target children. Language-comprehension items were
> also included as an index of teachers' language ability.

Merrit, Ray. "Self-Concept and Achievement in Home Economics." JOURNAL
OF HOME ECONOMICS 63 (January 1971): 38-40.

> It is assumed in the article that home economics classes can be
> used to develop positive self-pictures of students, especially those
> of average and below-average ability. Merrit feels that home eco-
> nomics affords the less intelligent individual with a more positive
> self-concept by combining practical application with studied con-
> cepts as different from purely academic courses. Through this com-
> bination, the home economics teacher is able to guide students into
> activities that bring out their abilities while playing down their
> limitations.

Miller, Douglas R. "School-Related Attitudes of Inner-City Junior High Students." Paper presented at the American Educational Research Association, New
Orleans, Louisiana, February 1973. (ED 076 723)

> Using an attitude survey, this study was done to find out more about
> the attitudes toward school held by inner-city children.

Miller, Harry B. "Reading and the Urban Child." Paper presented at the
Lehigh University Reading Conference, Bethlehem, Pennsylvania, 27 March
1971. (ED 051 961)

> Educators recognize the urban disadvantaged child presents unique
> problems to the schools, and few effective programs have been pro-
> vided for him. Some of the things mentioned which can be of bene-
> fit are: (1) effective programs beginning early in order to intervene
> with the language growth, (2) provision of appropriate realistic ma-
> terials, and (3) the teachers understanding the strength and weak-
> nesses of students, recognizing their language is often more differ-
> ent than deficient.

Miller, Harry L. PATTERNS OF EDUCATIONAL USE OF A TELEVISED PUBLIC
AFFAIRS PROGRAM. A STUDY OF A METROPOLIS--CREATOR OR DESTROYER.
New York: New York University, 1966. (ED 010 545)

> A national survey with a case-study approach was undertaken to de-
> termine the educational outcomes of broadcasting a public affairs,
> educational television (ETV) program.

Mink, Oscar G., and Kaplan, Bernard A. AMERICA'S PROBLEM YOUTH--
EDUCATION AND GUIDANCE OF THE DISADVANTAGED. Scranton, Pa.:
International Textbook Co., 1970.

> This publication is the result of a series of workshops designed for
> school personnel in Scranton desiring to improve educational programs
> for disadvantaged youth and potential dropouts. This information is
> presented in collective paper form.

Mitchell, Charles. "The Culturally Deprived--A Matter of Concern." CHILD-
HOOD EDUCATION 38 (May 1962): 412-20.

> Many large cities across the nation have concentrated areas of fami-
> lies whose children are severely hampered in their schooling by a
> combination of community, home, and school conditions. This is a
> report of a project in the Detroit public schools designed to allevi-
> ate some of these problems.

MODEL PROGRAMS, COMPENSATORY EDUCATION. PROJECT CONQUEST,
EAST ST. LOUIS, ILLINOIS. Palo Alto, Calif.: American Institutes for Research in the Behavioral Sciences, 1972. (ED 067 629)

> Project Conquest served 1,089 children in four "reading programs"
> (grades one, two, and three) and three "reading clinics" (grades
> four, five, and six). The objectives were: (1) to raise reading
> ability of mentally-able disadvantaged children so that they can
> function successfully in regular classrooms, (2) to improve their
> self-concepts and academic aspirations, and (3) to train regular
> classroom teachers in remedial reading techniques.

Mundstuk, Jay, and Kuzmack, Linda. SPECIAL SOCIAL STUDIES CLASS UNDER
MODEL SCHOOL PROGRAM OF THE WASHINGTON, D.C. PUBLIC SCHOOL
SYSTEM. FINAL REPORT. Washington, D.C.: Metropolitan Washington Plan-
ning and Housing Association, 1969. (ED 040 897)

> The report summarizes the background, objectives, developmental
> work, conclusions, and recommendations of Cardozo High School's
> urban problems program.

Muso, Barbara. "The Importance of Cumulative Records." EDUCATION 87
(April 1967): 488-90.

> This article stresses the need for careful and wise use of student
> records. A guide sheet for examining cumulative records is included.

THE NATIONAL URBAN COALITION RIGHT TO READ PROJECT, PHASE 2,
PRODUCTION AND DISSEMINATION OF PARENTS' KITS AND MANUALS.
FINAL REPORT. Washington, D. C.: National Urban Coalition, 1975. (ED 112
347)

The first section of this final report consists of a discussion of the production and dissemination of parents' kits and manuals. This section is followed by both a report on the pilot phase of the project and a report on the dissemination phase. The latter half of the document consists of lists of Right To Read Project participants, chief state school officers, directors of the Education for Parenthood Program, and Child and Family Resource Program contact people, as well as an example of what one nonparticipating coalition did with respect to distribution of the Right To Read "Recipes for Reading."

Nelson, Margaret. "Innovations in Urban Secondary Schools." SCHOOL RE-VIEW 84 (February 1976): 213-31.

This article reported the results of a survey of principals of 670 schools in all cities of the United States with a population of over 300,000 on their attitudes about the educational worth of a wide variety of educational innovations.

Nomland, Ella Kube, et al. EVALUATING OURSELVES IN HEAD START. Los Angeles: Greater Los Angeles Community Action Agency, 1973. (ED 109 141)

This Head Start evaluation system has a broad-based input and has been field tested. It includes evaluation schedules for the follow-ing components: education (bilingual education, bicultural educa-tion, education for handicapped children, educational facilities), health, social services, mental health, parent involvement, training and career development, nutrition, volunteers (other than parents), and administration.

North, Robert D. EVALUATION REPORT FOR THE ESEA TITLE III PROJECT, SOUTH BRONX MULTI-PURPOSE SUPPLEMENTARY EDUCATIONAL CENTER. Brooklyn: New York City Board of Education, 1968. (ED 026 690)

The purpose of this project was (1) to enhance the self-image of minority-group students, (2) to encourage development of their ar-tistic talent, and (3) to increase school-community cooperation.

Nunan, Desmond James. "A Study of Pupil Achievement and Attitude in a Multi-Neighborhood School." Ed.D. dissertation, University of Pennsylvania, 1969.

This study focused on the aspects of achievement and student atti-tudes with a multineighborhood school. The findings did not indi-cate significant differences in achievement but did suggest there were no detrimental effects noted. This study provides an examina-tion of issues closely concerned with transfer of children in urban schools for the purpose of school integration.

Ogbu, John U. THE NEXT GENERATION: AN ETHNOGRAPHY OF EDU-CATION IN AN URBAN NEIGHBORHOOD. New York: Academic Press, 1974. (ED 091 481)

This book is about education in Burgherside, a low-income neighborhood in Stockton, California. The study probes the reasons for many children from the neighborhood failing in the public schools.

Oliver, Albert I. "Partnership in Urban Education: An Alternative School." NASSP BULLETIN 59 (February 1975): 77-78.

A case study of a large Philadelphia high school spinning off some alternative units in an attempt to humanize learning for its predominantly black student population.

Ornstein, Allan C. RACE AND POLITICS IN SCHOOL/COMMUNITY ORGANIZATIONS. Pacific Palisades, Calif.: Goodyear, 1974.

This book reviews the behavior of school administrators to get their institution into programs which have funds available. These programs, rather than helping the poor, have often been carried out at their expense. Ornstein discusses such topics as: the researcher and the black community, return to racial quotas, and black nationalism. He devotes one entire chapter to "the rich." Ornstein's antiliberal views do not prevent him from speaking to some vital problem-solving concerns.

_____. "Techniques and Fundamentals for Teaching the Disadvantaged." THE JOURNAL OF NEGRO EDUCATION 36 (Spring 1967): 136-45.

Ornstein's teaching experience has been in city schools, but his suggestions have broad application. Planning, development of classroom routine, and discipline are emphasized.

_____. URBAN EDUCATION: STUDENT UNREST, TEACHER BEHAVIORS, AND BLACK POWER. Columbus, Ohio: Charles E. Merrill Publishing Co., 1972.

The contents of this book are as follows: Chapter 1, "The Disadvantaged: Overview and Trends," provides a brief synopsis of some of the major factors related to educating the disadvantaged. Chapter 2, "Emerging Youth Deprivation," examines two groups of students--middle- and upper-middle-class white students and black students of all classes--who seemed to most dissonant and active among all the student subgroups. Chapter 3, "Why Ghetto Teachers Fail," outlines the ways in which the teachers are victimized by their improper training, their students, their supervisors, the school system, and professors of education. Chapter 4, "Teacher Training for Ghetto Schools," develops a modest plan for improving teacher training, specifically for teachers of the disadvantaged. Chapter 5, "Myths of Integration, 'Liberalism' and Research on Blacks."

Palomares, Uvaldo H. SPECIAL NEEDS OF MEXICAN-AMERICANS: PROJECT DESIGN. EDUCATIONAL NEEDS. Fresno, Calif.: Fresno City Unified School District, 1968. (ED 038 765)

The major conclusion of this study is that a negative self-image exists among Mexican-American students and that negative school conditions surround them. Recommended changes in the attitudes of educators and educational procedures are outlined.

Passow, A. Harry, ed. URBAN EDUCATION IN THE 1970'S: REFLECTIONS AND A LOOK AHEAD. New York: Teachers College Press, Columbia University, 1971.

Nine authors contributed to this work, Kenneth B. Clark, Martin Deutsch, Miriam Goldberg, Vernon F. Haubrich, Robert J. Havighurst, Carl L. Marburger, Mel Ravitz, Alan Wilson, and A. Harry Passow. The overall concern is the increasing problems in urban education. This appears to be an effect of large programmatic efforts being made but based on some faulty assumptions. Many of the past failures of urban school reform relates to mismanagement.

Peelle, Carolyn Curtiss. "Where Children Learn: Breaking the Myth of Failure in Urban Education." Ed.D. dissertation, University of Massachusetts, 1972.

This study concerns the failure of the public education system to educate poor and minority Americans. The processes and problems as well as the prospects for urban education are focused upon here. The myths in education which serve to perpetuate these failures are identified. These are (1) the phenomenon of "blaming the victim," (2) the assumption that integration cannot work, and (3) the assumption that private citizens and professionals cannot change the system. The analysis reflects on the successes which dispute these myths.

THE PERSONALIZED CURRICULUM PROGRAM. Flint, Mich.: Flint Board of Education, 1964. (ED 002 393)

The potential dropout can be identified in kindergarten. His background, environment, and attitude prophesy his failure. Characteristics of potential dropouts include lack of interest, severe retardation in reading, and withdrawal tendencies. More than six hundred homes were visited by four trained social workers. Objectives were to obtain permission to place each pupil in the program and to gain insight into the families, their goals for their children, the values they place on education, and possible ways of upgrading the family through efforts in adult education.

PLANNING AND OPERATION OF AN EDUCATIONAL PARK. FINAL REPORT. Grand Rapids, Mich.: Grand Rapids Public Schools, 1971. (ED 070 201)

This report documents a three-year pilot project where juniors and seniors from public and nonpublic schools were transported to facilities in the central downtown areas for special courses under the umbrella of an educational park. For various reasons, these were courses not available at the individual schools. Also available in the program was a school for pregnant teenagers.

PRESCHOOL PROGRAM, ESEA TITLE I, 1973-74 SCHOOL YEAR. EVALUA-
TION REPORT. Saginaw, Mich.: Saginaw Public Schools, 1974. (ED 101 847)

> This is an evaluation report of a preschool program which served
> 403 children during the 1973-74 school year and was designed to
> prepare disadvantaged four-year-olds for entry into kindergarten.
> The program closely followed Piagetian theory and included preser-
> vice and inservice teaching training.

PROBLEMS PERCEIVED BY EDUCATIONAL LEADERSHIP: PROJECT DESIGN,
INTERAGENCY PLANNING FOR URBAN EDUCATION NEEDS. No. 6.
Fresno, Calif.: Fresno City Unified School District, 1968. (ED 038 748)

> This report is one in a series of needs assessment publications that
> comprise the initial phase for Project Design, an ESEA Title III
> project administered by the Fresno City Unified School District.
> This report summarizes educational problems of Fresno as they were
> perceived by district educational leaders.

PROJECT ASSIST: A PROGRAM TO MOTIVATE HIGH SCHOOL GRADUATES
TO ACQUIRE REMEDIAL EDUCATION AND TEST-TAKING SKILL TO QUALIFY
FOR EMPLOYMENT. Atlanta: National Urban League, Southern Regional Of-
fice, 1968.

> Project Assist was implemented in the six southern states of Florida,
> Georgia, Alabama, Mississippi, Tennessee, and South Carolina.
> The project focused on a target population of high school graduates
> and college dropouts between the ages of sixteen and thirty-five
> years. The goals were to break down various barriers to equal em-
> ployment opportunities, and to assist the participants to become
> more competitive in test-taking skills required for upgrading in their
> present employment or in obtaining entry-level jobs.

PROJECT EMERGE, DAYTON, OHIO. 1972-1973 FINAL EVALUATION RE-
PORT. Dayton: Dayton City School District, 1973. (ED 091 476)

> Project Emerge's major objectives are to reduce the dropout rate in
> grades nine through twelve, decrease absenteeism, and improve the
> students' academic performance and attitude toward school. Although
> it appears to have been rather successful, the objectives that were
> met seem to be related more to changes in board policy and the
> courts than in the efforts of the project.

PROVIDENCE EDUCATIONAL CENTER: AN EXEMPLARY PROJECT. Washington, D.C.: National Institute of Law Enforcement and Criminal Justice, 1974.
(ED 103 553)

> This is a handbook which provides the information needed to de-
> velop an alternative to incarceration in a training school similar
> to the Providence Educational Center (PEC) in St. Louis, Missouri.

READING: A STATEMENT OF POLICY AND PROPOSED ACTION; POSITION PAPER, NO. 12. Albany: New York State Education Department, 1971. (ED 076 974)

> This position paper outlines the essential characteristics of a reading program which will enable the schools of the state of New York to eliminate functional illiteracy among thousands of elementary and secondary students, and to attain the ultimate goal of reading education.

Reich, Carol. PRESCHOOL EDUCATION FOR INNER-CITY CHILDREN: PRELIMINARY RESULTS OF AN EXPERIMENTAL MONTESSORI PROGRAMME. Toronto: Toronto Board of Education, Research Department, 1971. (ED 066 219)

> Early results from a Montessori nursery program initiated in Toronto, Canada, in 1971, to help inner-city children prepare for formal education indicate that the mothers of the fifteen three and four-year-old children were pleased with the program. A study of the children's characteristics suggested that caution should be exerted in extrapolating the findings from other so-called disadvantaged children to inner-city children in one's own city.

REPORT ON URBAN VOCATIONAL EDUCATION. Washington, D.C.: National Advisory Council on Vocational Education, 1974. (ED 110 603)

> The National Advisory Council on Vocational Education conducted hearings in Washington, D.C., Pittsburgh, Atlanta, Los Angeles, and Houston, to gather information on the status of vocational education in urban areas. The report summarizes the testimony of the hearings, and identifies several common urban problems.

Resnik, Henry S. "Innovation is Tradition in West Harlem." SATURDAY REVIEW 55 (August 1972): 50-53.

> A husband-wife teaching team defies the rules of failure by giving their students a chance to fight the system.

Riessman, Frank. "The Overlooked Positives of Disadvantaged Groups." In THE DISADVANTAGED CHILD: ISSUES AND INNOVATIONS, edited by Joe L. Frost and Glenn R. Hawkes, pp. 51-57. Boston, Mass.: Houghton Mifflin Co., 1966.

> An aspect of the disadvantaged, often overlooked, is that they have strengths which should be capitalized upon in the teaching-learning process. Their possible strengths are reviewed.

Roberts, Dennis L. II. "Transforming Urban Life and Urban Education." EDUCATION TECHNOLOGY 10 (October 1970): 9-10.

> Roberts provides a brief discussion of the failure of politicians and educators to effectively deal with the urban crisis.

Robinson, Harry William. "The Development of a Coordinated Program of Health Education--Utilizing Community, Neighborhood, and Social Resources Leading Toward the Improvement of the East Park Elementary School and Its Neighborhood." Ph.D. dissertation, Harvard University, 1963.

Rocco, Alfonse M. "The Day They Turned the Showers On or, Understanding Values in Urban Education." ENGLISH JOURNAL 64 (April 1975): 35-37.

> This article discusses the cultural gap, the reasons for it and attempts to understand this phenomenon. To accomplish this Rocco reviews the psychological pressures, economic pressures, and the social class separations. He concludes that the complex interaction of pressures and the separation of social and economic classes are related to the cultural gap which exists and continues to grow.

Sankar, Milton Mellanauth Sarusudeer. "A Comparison of Two Methods of Increasing and Maintaining Reading Speed, Accuracy, Vocabulary and Comprehension Among Sixth-Grade Pupils in a Culturally Disadvantaged Neighborhood." Ph.D. dissertation, Indiana State University, 1973.

> This study involved a population of 58 sixth graders in a culturally-disadvantaged neighborhood. The two methods used were the Educational Development Laboratory tachistoscope and the EDL controlled reader, and the basal reader method. The results of the study indicate statistical significance for the measures taken by the machine, or EDL reader group. Measures of retention, reading speed, and vocabulary favored the EDL method.

Schenberg, Samuel, et al. A DISCOVERY WALK IN NATURAL SCIENCE. New York: American Museum of Natural History, 1975. (ED 106 067)

> This booklet is the correlated script for a forty-eight-frame color filmstrip designed to expand the environmental experiences of urban school children and their teachers.

Schwartz, Henrietta S., and McCampbell, James. "Staff Development in Low Power Transactional Organizations: The Administration of an Experimental Program in Urban Education." Paper presented at the American Educational Research Association, Chicago, Illinois, April 1974. (ED 091 486)

> Four common patterns have emerged from investigations of programs effective in preparing personnel for inner-city schools. This paper is a discussion of staff development and examines the conditions for adapting and implementing a transactional leadership style. The program is the Ford Training and Placement Program, a six-year experimental program undertaken by the University of Chicago and the Chicago Public Schools.

Schweitzer, Paul, et al. EVALUATION OF STATE URBAN EDUCATION PROGRAMS, DISTRICT 10. NEW YORK CITY, BOARD OF EDUCATION, 1970-

1971 SCHOOL YEAR. Albany: New York State Education Department, 1971.
(ED 059 339)

> The administrative component provides personnel and services for
> the planning, implementing, and supervising of all state urban edu-
> cation programs and for the coordination of activities of all partic-
> ipating groups. The Strengthening Basic Skills Program in junior
> high schools has been recycled from the 1969-70 school year. The
> Multi-Sensory Program, also recycled, provides seven schools with
> specific equipment and instructional materials used in remediation.

Seif, Elliot, and Harwood, Fred. "Urban Problems and Urban Education: Some
Thoughts and Curriculum Ideas." SOCIAL STUDIES 66 (January-February 1975):
7-10.

> The techniques, activities, and strategies focusing on the problems
> and concerns of urban Americans are suggested for use in elemen-
> tary grades to prepare students to cope with inner-city residence.
> They include a problem inventory, circle meetings, role playing,
> leadership training, physical and craft education as well as career,
> legal, and economic education.

Shalmo, Margaret. DRUGS AND YOU. GRADE FIVE, UNIT THREE, 5.3.
COMPREHENSIVE SOCIAL STUDIES CURRICULUM FOR THE INNER CITY.
Youngstown, Ohio: Youngstown Board of Education, 1971. (ED 104 786)

> This fifth grade unit is one of a sequential learning series from the
> Focus on Inner City Social Studies Project developed in accordance
> with the needs and problems of an urban society.

Shaw, Fredrick. "Educating Culturally Deprived Youth in Urban Centers."
PHI DELTA KAPPAN 45 (November 1963): 91-97.

> This article discusses the social origins of current problems in ur-
> ban education. In this context it describes such interventions as
> a pilot project in the Detroit public schools and New York City's
> High Horizons Project. These projects are characterized by (1) the
> use of specialized educational consultants and smaller class size,
> (2) community and parental involvement, and (3) the availability
> of special funds.

Singleton, John. "Cross-Culture Approaches to Research on Minority Group Education. Paper presented at the 68th annual meeting of the American Anthropo-
logical Association, New Orleans, Louisiana, 21 November 1969. (ED 040 245)

> Comparative studies of education, discrimination, and poverty in
> cross-cultural context are held as contributing towards a better un-
> derstanding of the social nature of poverty and the complex pro-
> cesses of cultural transmission, continuity, and change. Seven strat-
> egies or models of research are suggested.

Smilansky, Sara. THE EFFECTS OF SOCIODRAMATIC PLAY ON DISADVAN-
TAGED PRESCHOOL CHILDREN. New York: John Wiley and Sons, 1968.

> This study is a compilation of many authorities' particular knowledge
> and experience with the disadvantaged child.

Smith, Jeffrey K., and Wick, John W. "Practical Problems of Attempting to
Implement a Mastery Learning Program in a Large City School System." Paper
presented at the annual meeting of the American Educational Research Association, San Francisco, California, 19 April 1976. (ED 123 563)

> Low reading achievement in the Chicago public schools spurred the
> development of a mastery approach reading package. This approach
> assumes that in time any student can achieve the level of the bright-
> est student. Implementation of a mastery program in urban areas
> presents special problems, including diversity of student backgrounds,
> limitations of time and space, and varying degrees of teacher ex-
> pertise.

Smith, Louis M., and Geoffrey, William. THE COMPLEXITIES OF AN URBAN
CLASSROOM; AN ANALYSIS TOWARD A GENERAL THEORY OF TEACHING.
New York: Holt, Rinehart and Winston, 1968.

> The goal of this book is to describe the real world of the slum
> classroom and build a more general theory of teaching. The au-
> thors identify teacher decision-making processes, development of
> social structure, the establishment of roles, expectations, beliefs,
> and norms. They classify teacher behavior according to process.
> This work has significance for those who believe that educational
> change must start in the classroom.

SOCIAL MALADJUSTMENT: BEHAVIOR CHANGE AND EDUCATION, PRO-
CEEDINGS OF THE FIFTH ANNUAL CONFERENCE ON URBAN EDUCATION.
New York: Yeshiva University, 1966. (ED 021 894)

> These proceedings contain four papers and commentaries by scholars
> on the problems of the socially disadvantaged child in the urban
> school. The papers discuss (1) cognitive development and psycho-
> pathology in the urban environment, (2) an experimental approach
> to the remediation of the conduct disorders of children, (3) juve-
> nile delinquency in the urban schools, and (4) the effect of pov-
> erty on the education of the urban child.

SPECIAL PROJECT IN URBAN READING TESTS, COMPONENT 1: PRE-READ-
ING SKILLS BATTERY. New York: Center for Urban Education, 1971. (ED 096
638)

> This skills battery, ready for experimental edition publication, was
> designed as an urban oriented testing instrument. It is intended
> for use both as a screening device and diagnostic tool to provide
> the teacher with information on the child's strengths and weak-
> nesses in specific prereading skills areas.

Streets, Virgus Otis. SPECIAL NEEDS OF NEGROS: PROJECT DESIGN. EDU-CATIONAL NEEDS. Fresno, Calif.: Fresno City Unified School District, 1968. (ED 038 766)

> This study assesses the special learning needs of black students and adults. Interviews were focused on the day-to-day operation of the school.

Stroud, Marion. GREEN POWER: HOUSING GRADE TWO. UNIT TWO. 2.2. COMPREHENSIVE SOCIAL STUDIES CURRICULUM FOR THE INNER CITY. Youngstown, Ohio: Youngstown Board of Education, 1971. (ED 104 777)

> As part of the second-grade curriculum of introductory economics, this unit of the Focus on Inner City Social Studies Series explores housing and communities. The unit provides an active study in which children explore and probe into community conditions. They experiment with methods of improving their own environment and develop self-esteem in belonging to groups working to raise community standards.

A STUDY OF URBAN EDUCATION. A REPORT. Springfield: Illinois State School Problems Commission, 1969. (ED 030 179)

> To obtain a clearer understanding of the problems of urban education in Illinois, a committee of seven state legislators and fourteen lay citizens conducted this study.

SUPERVISOR'S MANUAL. YOUTH TUTORING YOUTH. New York: National Commission on Resources for Youth, 1968.

> Two programs, based on the concept of youth tutoring younger children with benefit to both, were conducted by the National Commission on Resources for Youth NCRY, and the respective school systems of Newark and Philadelphia during the summer of 1967.

Taba, Hilda, and Elkins, Deborah. TEACHING STRATEGIES FOR THE CULTURALLY DISADVANTAGED. Chicago: Rand McNally and Co., 1966.

> Though based on teaching efforts applied to children in the city slum, many of the children were recent immigrants from the South, with the background and technique descriptions broadly generalized. Of particular interest is material on diagnosing gaps and abilities which appears in chapter three.

Thomas, Thomas C. EDUCATIONAL POLICY FOR THE INNER-CITY. DRAFT. Menlo Park, Calif.: Stanford Research Institute, Educational Policy Research Center, 1967. (ED 033 435)

> Most of the important educational issues for the country are represented in problems of urban education. This report concentrates on

one of the practical issues for the urban education policymaker--
education policy for the poor minority child who lives in the inner
city.

THREE CONFERENCES: URBANIZATION, WORK AND EDUCATION (CHICAGO,
ILLINOIS, APRIL 1967); YOUTH IN A CHANGING SOCIETY (CLEVELAND,
OHIO, MAY 1967); TEACHER EDUCATION IN A NEW CONTEXT (MADISON,
WISCONSIN, MAY 1967); PROJECT REPORT FOUR, THE NDEA NATIONAL
INSTITUTE FOR ADVANCED STUDY IN TEACHING DISADVANTAGED YOUTH.
Washington, D.C.: American Association of Colleges for Teacher Education,
1968. (ED 033 893)

> This booklet contains selected papers from three conferences which
> had common objectives: to enable federal, state, and local offi-
> cials to study the complexity of legal, social, economic, and psy-
> chological constraints on youth as well as the agencies created by
> these laws; to review the critical factors in urbanization, their re-
> lation to disadvantaged youth, and the impact on society of the ur-
> banizing community; to examine the implication of changing pat-
> terns of work, living, and recreation for agencies and individuals
> responsible for youth, especially those who control the education
> of youth and the preparation of teachers; and to examine alterna-
> tive strategies of action--legislative, educational, and social--
> which could serve as guides for responsible public officials.

Tokmakian, Harold. LONG-RANGE SCHOOL SITE LOCATION PLAN: PRO-
JECT DESIGN. INTERAGENCY PLANNING FOR URBAN EDUCATIONAL
NEEDS. Fresno, Calif.: Fresno City Unified School District, 1969. (ED 038
774)

> This publication contains an analysis of the factors that must be
> considered in locating new school sites for the Fresno district, as
> well as the principles and standards related to community planning
> and school site location.

Trockman, Mitchell D. INSTRUCTIONAL MATERIALS CENTER, PROJECT DI-
RECTOR'S REPORT: 1969-1970. Minneapolis, Minn.: Minneapolis Public
Schools, 1970. (ED 068 899)

> The Instructional Materials Center (IMC) originated in association
> with the development of a course to train teachers in specific tech-
> niques for teaching reading and the use of a wide range of multi-
> sensory reading materials.

U. S. Congress. House. Committee on Education and Labor. OVERSIGHT HEAR-
ING ON ELEMENTARY AND SECONDARY EDUCATION. HEARINGS ON H.R.
6179, H.R. 7796, H.R. 12695, AND RELATED PROPOSALS. 92d Cong., 2d
Sess., 1972. (ED 070 171)

> This document contains statements, letters, articles, and supplemen-
> tal materials submitted by congressmen and educational representa-

tives on categorical aid and general aid to education. The materials cover a broad spectrum of federal programs. Many of the articles and statements focus on the problems of urban education.

U. S. Congress. Senate. Select Committee on Equal Educational Opportunity. EQUAL EDUCATIONAL OPPORTUNITY. HEARINGS ON PART 13--QUALITY AND CONTROL OF URBAN SCHOOLS. 92d Cong., 1st sess., 1971.

The committee held hearings on the quality and control of urban schools (Summer 1971). The testimony of the various witnesses is recorded. Among the witnesses are professors of education, community leaders, and administrators of urban schools. The appendix includes material submitted by the witnesses and relevant newspaper articles.

URBAN EDUCATION PROJECT, ESEA TITLE V-505, MID-ATLANTIC REGIONAL INTERSTATE PLANNING PROJECT. Hartford, Conn.: State Department of Education, 1971. (ED 070 751)

This is a report on urban education projects from Connecticut, Delaware, New Jersey, New York, and Pennsylvania. It describes the implementation of individual state programs to improve the quality of urban education, and also includes a report on the implementation of the recommendations made in "The Urban Teacher, A Preliminary Report."

Vail, Edward O. "Inner-City Reading Programs Can Work." AUDIOVISUAL INSTRUCTION 16 (November 1971): 51-52.

This is a report of a study conducted at Los Angeles Carver Junior High School. The study is concerned with Formula Phonics (a word attack process which has been reduced to a single formula) as a way to teach remedial reading. The results are impressive and offer the reader some thoughts on this approach.

Van Strat, Georgena. "The Reading Problem in Urban Schools: Who Has It and What Has Been Done About It?" Ed.D. dissertation, University of Massachusetts, 1975. (ED 110 938)

The purpose of this paper is the identification of ingredients of successful urban reading programs in order to effect an increase in reading achievement in urban schools. An historical-sociological framework is established, pertinent literature is reviewed, various topics are discussed and reading programs and practices which have achieved measurable success are described. The Career Opportunities Program at the University of Massachusetts is discussed as an effective model for urban teacher training.

VOCATIONAL EDUCATION IN THE FIVE LARGE CITIES OF CALIFORNIA. MAJOR URBAN CENTERS VOCATIONAL EDUCATION PROJECT. Berkeley and Los Angeles: University of California Press, 1969. (ED 041 113)

Vocational education in large urban areas is a key element in meeting the demands of economic, social, and technological change. The five major California urban centers included in this study are Long Beach, Los Angeles, Oakland, San Diego, and San Francisco.

Walsh, Huber M., ed. AN ANTHOLOGY OF READING IN ELEMENTARY SOCIAL STUDIES. SOCIAL STUDIES READINGS FOUR. Washington, D.C.: National Council for the Social Studies, 1971. (ED 058 130)

There are fifty articles in this anthology drawn from the ELEMENTARY EDUCATION SUPPLEMENT OF SOCIAL EDUCATION. The purpose is to provide inspiration and worthwhile suggestions for upgrading social studies instruction in the elementary school.

Wang, Margaret C., et al. PEP IN THE FRICK ELEMENTARY SCHOOL: INTERIM EVALUATION REPORT 1969-1970. Pittsburgh: Pittsburgh University, Pennsylvania Learning Research and Development Center, 1974. (ED 104 911)

The Primary Education Project (PEP) is concerned with the development and evaluation of a model of individualized education for young children which would be suitable for implementation in public schools at the preschool through primary grade levels. It is concerned with curriculum, classroom organization, teacher training, staff development, and work with parents.

Warden, Sandra A. THE LEFTOUT DISADVANTAGED CHILDREN IN HETER - OGENEOUS SCHOOLS. New York: Holt, Rinehart and Winston, 1968.

More than good intentions and financial support are needed for effective compensatory education. The author believes that cooperative planning, coordinated activities, and a great deal of research and training seem necessary, all of which should begin with a thorough understanding of the problems of socioculturally disadvantaged children.

Watkins, Clyde P. "Teaching the Future Citizen of the Inner City." INDIANA SOCIAL STUDIES QUARTERLY 24 (August 1971): 21-25.

Inner-city youth must be made aware of the problems confronting them on an individual level, the social factors which have brought these problems about, the facts about the constitutional relationships between citizen and government, and, finally, the uses of citizen power.

Watson, D.R. "Urban Education and Cultural Competence: Competing Theoretical Models in Social Science." URBAN EDUCATION 8 (April 1973): 20-40.

Watson appraises the assumptions underlying much of the work in urban education by reviewing the deficit system model, the cultural pluralism model, and the radical vanguard model, and by proposing an alternate competencies model drawing on ethnomethodology for theoretical justification.

Watson, Dorothy, et al., eds. THREE DEVELOPMENTAL MODELS DESIGNED FOR THE EDUCATION OF LOW INCOME CHILDREN. Kansas City: University of Missouri-Kansas City, 1970. (ED 100 868)

This paper presents three different educational models for inner-city children: (1) a learning by doing program, (2) the development and study of a reading center in an inner-city elementary school, and (3) a model program designed to bring together children from inner and outer Kansas City areas.

Wheeler, Robert R. "Statement Made to the United States Senate Select Committee on Equal Educational Opportunity." 15 July 1971. (ED 055 746)

Using the successful reading program of Kansas City, Missouri, as a basis for discussion, the author makes suggestions for future federal legislation and for administration of federally-funded educational programs.

Wilcohon, Reba, ed. DEMONSTRATION AND RESEARCH CENTER FOR EARLY EDUCATION (DARCEE). Nashville: Demonstration and Research Center for Early Education, George Peabody College for Teachers, 1968. (ED 107 384)

This booklet describes the activities of the Demonstration and Research Center for Early Education (DARCEE). The purpose of DARCEE is to answer questions about cognitive and emotional development of the young child through basic and applied research. Emphasis is on overcoming the learning deficiencies of disadvantaged children using structured instruction and a programmed reinforcement schedule in the classroom, as well as intervention programs in the community.

Wilder, Amos. "Client Criticism of Urban Schools: How Valid?" PHI DELTA KAPPAN 51 (November 1969): 129-30.

The author defines the clients of the education system as the student, the parent, and the community. These clients are served by the professional administrators and teachers of urban schools. The services of these professionals are questioned in terms of benefits received by the clients. The author relates the concern of accountability with the sharing of responsibility for the performance of the delivery system. He questions the lack of initiative by educators to accept performance standards which are demanded of other professions by their clients.

Wildman, Louis. DISCIPLINARY PROBLEMS IN URBAN GHETTO SCHOOLS. Seattle, Wash.: School Information and Research Service, 1971. (ED 055 142)

This article describes the group dynamics of the inner-city school by focusing on hypothetical examples of teacher-peer group and student-peer group support. Also included is a discussion of possible ways for improving the educational environment.

Willis, David E., and Fiasca, Michael A. "An Experiment in Cooperative Inquiry: The Portland, Oregon TTT." JOURNAL OF TEACHER EDUCATION 26 (Fall 1975): 214-17.

The author discusses the use of the systematic method of inquiry into learning. The dynamics of the intended use of this method with ghetto students was highly successful in terms of the transfer of skills and knowledge. The key component in this methodology was the provision of continuing feedback for both student and teacher. The student's role was defined as that of a co-learner. This approach is discussed as an alternative to methods which are considered ineffectual by comparison.

Wisniewski, Richard, ed. TEACHING ABOUT LIFE IN THE CITY. Washington, D.C.: National Council for the Social Studies, 1972. (ED 069 594)

The purpose of this yearbook is to examine key aspects of American urban society, to identify issues that are central to all social studies instruction about the city, and to present specific ideas on how teachers can present these issues both inside and outside the classroom.

Wolff, Max. THE EDUCATIONAL PARK: A GUIDE TO ITS IMPLEMENTATION. New York: Center for Urban Education, 1970. (ED 040 228)

This book analyzes the "educational park" concept as an approach to the current crisis of the inner city and its public school system.

Zerr, Rita Gregorio. "A Comparative Analyses of Selected Variables and Responses of Preschool Children to Science--A Process Approach in New Orleans' Child Development Centers." Ph.D. dissertation, University of Southern Mississippi, 1970. (ED 092 320)

This report is a study to determine whether selected variables characterizing disadvantaged preschool children and teachers are related to achievement in a science--a process approach curriculum.

Section C

THE TRAINING AND RECRUITMENT OF TEACHERS

ABSTRACTS OF MIDWEST CENTER/SATELLITES FINAL PROGRAM REPORTS. Bloomington: Center for Research in Education, Indiana University, n.d. (ED 116 096)

> This document is a collection of six abstracts representing a summary of the activities of a three-year project supported by the Education Professions Development Act.

Alberty, Elsie J. INNOVATIVE UNDERGRADUATE TEACHER EDUCATION PROGRAMS. Columbus: Ohio State University, 1970. (ED 050 015)

> This is a description of twelve experimental or innovative teacher education programs at Ohio State University. Programs include urban teacher education, English for the inner city, development and evaluation of intermediate levels of industrial arts, microteaching of foreign languages, microteaching in social studies, middle elementary team teaching, training in early childhood and the disadvantaged, training of ghetto dropouts as educational technicians.

Amidon, Edmund J., and Rosenshine, Barak. "Interaction Analysis and Microteaching in an Urban Teacher Education Program. A Model for Skill Development in Teaching." Paper presented at the American Educational Research Association, Chicago, Illinois, February 1968. (ED 076 496)

> The proposed Skill Development in Teaching (SKIT) model is an attempt to combine significant aspects of interaction analysis and microteaching. An integral part of the SKIT program are the skill sessions, which emphasize various teaching behaviors to be practiced.

Anderson, Lowell D. A REPORT ON THE BALTIMORE CITY FUNDED PROJECT ON PROBLEMS OF URBAN VOCATIONAL SCHOOLS USING A CROSS-DISCIPLINE TEAM-TEACHING MODEL AT CARVER AND MERGENTHALER, SUMMER 1972. College Park: Maryland University, Department of Industrial Education, 1972. (ED 073 087)

This report summarizes a workshop for teachers of disadvantaged and handicapped students in vocational schools in the urban setting. Goals for the workshop represented both the affective and cognitive domains of teacher behavior modification.

Arrington, J. Don, and Cutter, Irene. "EPDA Comprehensive Intensified Teacher Training Project." INDIANA READING QUARTERLY 3 (January 1971): 23-24, 27.

Bailey, Stephen K. "The City as Classroom." Speech given at the annual convention of the New York State Council for the Social Studies, Buffalo, New York, 23 April 1971. (ED 049 983)

The author gives a rationale for utilizing the city as a place to learn. The city has many problems and although logistics require that we conduct most education in the school building, the author argues for putting our best brains to the task of bringing the city to the classroom and to exploiting the city as a classroom when appropriate.

Baptiste, Hansom P., Jr., and Meindl, Carmelita O. AN ANSWER TO A CHALLENGE: INNOVATION IN UNIVERSITY CURRICULUM. South Bend: Indiana University, 1971. (ED 062 932)

This paper discusses the development, implementation, and evaluation of a first-year action program designed to prepare urban people for careers in education.

Bernstein, Abraham. THE EDUCATION OF URBAN POPULATIONS. New York: Random House, 1967. (ED 032 366)

A new teacher-education text stresses the primacy of urban problems. Also emphasized is a new direction in the training and recruitment of teachers for urban schools.

Bess, Lorraine J., et al. URBAN ON-SITE TEACHER EDUCATION PREPARATION IN TEACHER EDUCATION CENTERS: BRUCE ELEMENTARY SCHOOL, SEATON ELEMENTARY SCHOOL, TRUESDELL ELEMENTARY SCHOOL. Washington, D.C.: District of Columbia Teachers College, 1971. (ED 077 916)

An inner-city, elementary teacher education program is presented. Some of the things the program focuses on are: (1) the acquisition of teaching techniques and skills in the urban learning setting, (2) the learning of theory together with reinforced practice in functional field experiences, and (3) the encouragement of continuous evaluation.

Bossone, Richard M. "Disadvantaged Teachers in Disadvantaged Schools." CONTEMPORARY EDUCATION 41 (February 1970): 183-85.

Bruno, James E. "Minority Group Involvement in Urban Teaching: A Design for Use of Noncredentialed Personnel in Regular Instructional Programs of Large Urban School Districts." EDUCATION AND URBAN SOCIETY 3 (November 1970): 41-70.

Buck, Benjamin. THE INTRODUCTORY URBAN EDUCATION PROGRAM. Mankato, Minn.: Mankato State College, School of Education, 1971. (ED 065 480)

> This program provides students with an intercultural, interdisciplinary, and interinstitutional educational program. Assignment is made to a classroom teacher, with a specified number of hours per week required with social agencies and community projects. Certain courses such as psychology, sociology, political science, and human growth and development are also required.

Button, Warren. "Teacher Education for the Inner City: Suppositions and Reservations." URBAN EDUCATION 4 (October 1969): 195-200.

Clothier, Grant M., and Hudgins, Bryce B. UNIQUE CHALLENGES OF PREPARING TEACHERS FOR INNER-CITY SCHOOLS: PROGRESS AND PROSPECTS. Washington, D.C.: ERIC Clearinghouse on Teacher Education; Kansas City, Mo.: Mid-Continent Regional Educational Laboratory, 1971. (ED 056 971)

> During the 1960s there was growing awareness that without competent teachers who could understand the problems of ghetto life there would be further deterioration of the educational process. The first half of this paper traces the growth of this awareness by looking at teacher education programs and the writings of leading educators. The second part deals with future prospects for inner-city teacher education, challenges facing the teacher, economic factors affecting teacher supply and demand, and the desirable characteristics of inner-city teachers.

Comeaux, Pamela Harris. A FOLLOW-UP STUDY OF 1967-1970 COOPERATIVE URBAN TEACHER EDUCATION GRADUATES. Kansas City, Mo.: Mid-Continent Regional Educational Laboratory, 1971. (ED 100 925)

> The Cooperative Urban Teacher Education Program (CUTE) enrolled 295 volunteer teachers for one semester in their senior year of college and trained them in an inner-city school. The employment data of that program are provided.

Crim, Alonzo A. TECHNOLOGY FOR PRE-SERVICE AND IN-SERVICE TRAINING OF TEACHERS OF GHETTO CHILDREN. Washington, D.C.: Academy for Educational Development, 1970. (ED 039 739)

> Technology can best be applied in the preparation of teachers for the ghetto by evaluating current practices in teacher training and by using the results of this evaluation in applied and basic research. Some acute problems facing teacher education for ghetto schools include language barriers, cultural gaps, and teacher career patterns.

DUALITY IN SOCIETY: DUALITY IN TEACHER EDUCATION. Chicago: Northeastern Illinois University, 1971. (ED 074 016)

> A student teaching program was developed at Northeastern Illinois University to prepare the student to function in both the inner-city and outer-city settings. Five major aspects of the program were: cross assignment, group counseling, seminars, other backup experiences, and duality workshops.

Duff, William L., Jr., et al. "Teacher Retention and Student Performance in the Inner-Urban Elementary School." Paper presented at the annual meeting of the American Educational Research Association, New York, February 1971. (ED 047 074)

> The objective of this study is to identify the correlates of student performance and teacher retention in an inner-city elementary school district.

EDUCATION IN DISADVANTAGED URBAN AREAS: AN IN-SERVICE COURSE, JANUARY-MARCH, 1964. Boston: Boston Public Schools, 1964. (ED 023 707)

> This pamphlet contains the lectures delivered during an inservice course for staff in the Boston public schools to acquaint them with the characteristics of their black students.

Eland, Calvin. THE CULTURALLY DISADVANTAGED: A FIELD EXPERIENCE GUIDE. MATERIALS/ONE. Washington, D.C.: American Association of Colleges for Teacher Education and National Institute for Advanced Study in Teaching Disadvantaged Youth, 1968. (ED 080 497)

> This guide resulted from the work of fourteen colleges and universities in the Red River Valley Inter-Institutional Project. Some of the aims of the project were: (1) an awareness of the problems in teaching the disadvantaged, (2) the comparison of rural and urban disadvantaged youth, and (3) an exploration of teaching the disadvantaged and teaching in general.

Emeruwa, Leatrice. "Teaching Reading to the Inner-City Child." Paper presented at the International Reading Association Conference, Anaheim, California, 6 May 1970. (ED 044 249)

> This paper deals with the type of teacher needed to teach reading at all grade levels in urban schools. It also identifies the habits and attitudes necessary for success.

AN EVALUATION OF THE PROGRAM "SUPPORTIVE TRAINING FOR INEXPERIENCED AND NEW TEACHERS" (STINT) IN NEW YORK CITY SCHOOLS. New York: Institute for Educational Development, 1970. (ED 051 087)

> The STINT teacher training program was designed for inexperienced

teachers to gain support from experienced teachers who were on
100 percent release time to work with participants on a ratio of
approximately one to nine. The goals included: supportive services, development of teacher competency, development of effective methodologies, and methods to improve learning situations.
Instruments used in evaluation are included in this document.

EVALUATIVE ASSESSMENT OF EXEMPLARY PRE-SERVICE TEACHER TRAINING
FOR INNER-CITY ELEMENTARY TEACHERS. VOL. 5, MODELS OF TEACHER
TRAINING. Los Angeles: Contemporary Research, 1972.

This report was designed to assess exemplary preservice teacher
training programs for inner-city teachers.

Eve, Arthur W., et al. AN EVALUATION OF THE WASHINGTON, D.C.
URBAN STAFF DEVELOPMENT LABORATORY. Amherst: Massachusetts University, Institute for Governmental Services, 1973. (ED 088 872)

This is an evaluation of the Urban Staff Development Laboratory
Graduate Program. The project objective was to provide quality
education for youth living in the Model Cities Neighborhood in
Washington, D.C. by upgrading the competency of elementary and
secondary level teachers in the area.

A FINAL PROGRAM REPORT FROM INDIANA UNIVERSITY--INDIANAPOLIS
PUBLIC SCHOOLS INNER CITY COUNSELOR TRAINING PROJECT, 1971-1974.
Indianapolis: Indianapolis Public Schools; Bloomington: Indiana University,
1974. (ED 116 098)

Recognizing the need for improved, more flexible, more reality-
based training for pupil personnel workers, the Division of Foundations and Human Behavior, Indiana University, in conjunction with
the Department of Counseling and Guidance, formed a relationship with the Indianapolis Public Schools in order to seek out methods of improving pupil personnel service.

A FINAL PROGRAM REPORT FROM JANE ADDAMS SCHOOL OF SOCIAL
WORK. Urbana: The School-Community-Pupil-Training Program, University
of Illinois, 1971-1974. (ED 116 099)

This project tried to train a new kind of professional school social
worker who would work to improve the way school systems respond
to children, mainly minority children. The interns worked with
the school districts at the same time they were learning about school
social work to help alleviate problem areas.

Fractenberg, Paul L. EQUAL EMPLOYMENT OPPORTUNITIES IN THE NEW
YORK PUBLIC SCHOOLS: AN ANALYSIS AND RECOMMENDATIONS BASED
ON PUBLIC HEARINGS HELD JANUARY 25-29, 1971. New York: New York
City Commission on Human Rights, 1971. (ED 050 207)

This is a report on the analysis and recommendations based on public hearings designed to ascertain divergent views. The view of some was that the current system of selection is sound. However, in the view of others, there are certain fundamental flaws which cannot be completely corrected except by wholesale reform. Questioned were the rigid examination process, the recruiting of teachers, and the use of probationary periods.

Goldman, Harvey, and Lawson, Richard. "When Inner-City Teachers Are Given Free Time." JOURNAL OF NEGRO EDUCATION 40 (Winter 1971): 4-11.

Goodale, Ellen, comp. MULTICULTURAL TEACHER TRAINING. Boston: Boston Public Schools; Massachusetts University, Boston Institute for Learning and Teaching, 1974. (ED 103 522)

This paper deals with the inservice training programs for bilingual teachers of the Bilingual Department of the Boston Public Schools. Two points are of particular interest: (1) the shift from the piecemeal English-as-a-second-language program to the more comprehensive bilingual programs, and (2) the development of a process by which specific training needs could be identified and acted upon. The goals were to cooperatively develop, with individual schools, procedures for establishing effective bilingual education programs.

GOVERNORS STATE UNIVERSITY URBAN TEACHER EDUCATION PROGRAM. Park Forest South, Ill.: Governors State University, 1972. (ED 076 517)

Assuming student teachers must be knowledgeable about current socioeconomic factors in their working environment, the program aims at developing these competencies. It is oriented toward preparing teachers for urban schools.

Green, Robert L. CRISIS IN AMERICAN EDUCATION--A RACIAL DILEMMA. Washington, D.C.: U. S. Commission on Civil Rights, 1967. (ED 015 980)

American education has not yet sufficiently recognized the critical role of teaching quality and teachers' attitudes as instruments of social change. Unfortunately, data from a survey of ten major teacher training institutions show that they "are not realistically facing the problem of providing quality teachers for urban youth."

Gromfin, Annette M. INITIAL SYSTEMATIC MANAGEMENT DESIGN FOR TEACHER CORPS, CYCLE V, UNIVERSITY OF SOUTHERN CALIFORNIA, SCHOOL OF EDUCATION. Los Angeles: University of Southern California, School of Education, 1971. (ED 100 905)

This report of the initial systematic management design covers the two years of the program. Some of the objectives of the program are: (1) to train interns in depth to understand delinquent youth in the educational process, (2) to award a master's degree to each intern, and (3) to develop new relationships between correctional schools and inner-city schools.

Gross, Mary J., et al. COMBINED HUMAN EFFORTS IN EVALUATING ACHIEVEMENT AT THE WHEATLEY SCHOOL, WASHINGTON, D.C. Ed.D. Practicum, Nova University, 1974. (ED 102 666)

> The purpose of this practicum was to plan and implement a comprehensive development program for the staff, parents, and community at an inner-city elementary school serving a disadvantaged, segregated student population.

Haggett, William F. PHILADELPHIA URBAN EDUCATION NETWORK PROJECT: SECOND-YEAR FINAL REPORT. Philadelphia: Philadelphia School District, Office of Research and Evaluation, 1975. (ED 115 695)

> The Philadelphia Urban Education Network Project, a staff development project, deals with the problems of urban teachers and the needs of urban students. Progress was made (1974-75) in the following areas: (1) an increase in the use of individualized and small group instruction, (2) an increase in the use of affective approaches in instruction, (3) training of student-teachers in an urban setting, and (4) getting the community involved in various school activities.

HOME ECONOMICS AND THE DISADVANTAGED. Report of a workshop. DeKalb: Northern Illinois University, June 1970.

> This publication is the result of a twelve-day workshop held to improve the understanding of disadvantaged students and methods to use with them. The following topics were covered: (1) home economics and the educable mentally handicapped, (2) integration of the disadvantaged in suburban schools, (3) an example of a personal development unit for rural disadvantaged pupils, and (4) a child development curriculum guide for eighth graders in the inner city. An annotated bibliography is included.

Hunt, Paul R., and Rasef, Elving I. "Discipline: Function or Task?" In THE INNER CITY CLASSROOM: TEACHER BEHAVIOR, edited by Robert Strom, pp. 131-44. Columbus, Ohio: Charles E. Merrill Publishing Co., 1966.

> This article discusses ways a teacher can discipline a group of students who really have had no contact with an adult. Eliminating failure and providing honest appraisal, sincerity, and consistency are the suggestions the author gives for maintaining discipline.

Hyram, George H. URBAN ECONOMIC FACTORS IN EDUCATION: THE KNOWLEDGE BASE FOR PRE- AND IN-SERVICE EDUCATIONAL PERSONNEL. St. Louis, Mo.: St. Louis University, 1974.

This paper discusses two areas of knowledge that education professionals must develop to help resolve the crisis in the city and the
suburbs. One area concerns key urban economic factors affecting
elementary and secondary education. The second area of knowledge
concerns six special problems of the culturally disadvantaged that
teachers face.

Imhoof, Maurice. "The Preparation of Language Arts Teachers for Ghetto Schools."
Paper presented at the fourth annual TESOL convention, San Francisco, California,
18 March 1970. (ED 040 389)

Language arts teachers' evaluation of language abilities of ghetto
children is handicapped by a lack of academic preparation in urban dialects and the nature of language. Ghetto students need to
develop language skills which alternate between the dialects of
peers and family, and that of his teachers and books.

Kane, Candice Marie. "Factors Related to Teacher Open-mindedness as Measured by the Rokeach Dogmatism Scale and the Modified Kelly Exploration Questionnaire in a Neighborhood Undergoing Racial Change." Ph.D. dissertation,
Northwestern University, 1976.

This study used the Rokeach Dogmatism Scale to measure job satisfaction, teacher open-mindedness, and receptivity to change. Other
instruments used were the modified Kelly Exploration Questionnaire
and a personal data form. The results indicated there was a relationship between the Rokeach Dogmatism Scale and the Modified
Kelly Exploration Questionnaire. This relationship shows a high
degree of correlation. However, there were no indications that
job satisfaction was connected to any of the other variables.

Kaplan, Bernard A., et al. EDUCATING THE CULTURALLY DEPRIVED IN THE
GREAT CITIES. Bloomington, Ind.: Phi Delta Kappan, 1963. (ED 001 603)

A series of articles features the education of the culturally disadvantaged in urban areas. Subjects range from consideration of general issues to specific problems facing the inner-city teacher. In
one case a personal experience of a teacher living in a changing
neighborhood is described.

Knowles, Jerry, et al. "Peace Corps Veterans: An Approach to Urban Education." CONTEMPORARY EDUCATION 42 (October 1970): 35-38.

Krosky, Roy T. THE INNER CITY TEACHER EDUCATION PROGRAM. Greeley:
University of Northern Colorado, 1971.

This program emphasizes the preparation of prospective teachers for
working in urban schools whose populations are composed of children from culturally-diverse backgrounds. Besides class study

and student teaching, students take part in field trips, live-in experiences, and concentrated studies related to the offerings of the program.

Laurer, Linonel. "Training and Utilization of Administrators for Urban School Systems: The School District's Perspective." Paper presented at the annual convention of the American Association of School Administrators, Dallas, Texas, 21 February 1975. (ED 108 349)

Laurer describes the Philadelphia program for training urban school administrators. It showed success in meeting the needs of student unrest, racial confrontation, and under-representation of minority groups in leadership positions.

Lawson, James H. INNOVATION IN THE INNER CITY: A REPORT ON THE COOPERATIVE URBAN TEACHER EDUCATION PROGRAM. Kansas City, Mo.: Mid-Continent Regional Educational Laboratory, 1969.

This publication, the first in a series dealing with the Cooperative Urban Teacher Education Program, is an effort to introduce interested persons to a program which has tried to bring together a number of components into a closely integrated experience designed to equip teacher-education students with the skills needed to meet the heart-to-heart and mind-to-mind confrontations of the inner-city school with some prospect of success.

Lawson, James H., and McClernon, Francis M. SUMMARY OF THE CO-OPERATIVE URBAN TEACHER EDUCATION EVALUATION, 1968-1969. WORKING PAPER. Vol. 2, no. 1. Kansas City, Mo.: Mid-Continent Regional Educational Laboratory, 1969. (ED 043 600)

This second of a series of evaluation reports of the Cooperative Urban Teacher Education (CUTE) program covers 1968-69 and replicates portions of the 1967-68 evaluation, assesses the effects of the program, and provides recommendations for the program directors.

Linton, Thomas E. "An Alternative Teacher Training Model for Urban America-- The Teacher as a Social Systems Agent." Paper presented at the American Educational Research Association Conference, Chicago, Illinois, April 1972. (ED 062 490)

An alternative teacher-education model is proposed which places first priority on the actual training of teachers as well as administrators for the public schools. Some of the assumptions made are: (1) teacher training as such is the most important task that educators can effectively engage in, (2) value questions are of major and primary importance in the total educational process, and (3) the teacher's function is to develop human potential.

Littky, Dennis, and Bosley, Lenora. A CONTINGENCY MANAGEMENT PROGRAM IN URBAN SCHOOL CLASSROOMS. New York: Institute for the Advancement of Urban Education, 1970. (ED 041 966)

> The program was implemented in the Ocean Hill Brownsville Demon-
> stration School District. It was designed to train teachers and para-
> professionals to work within the present school system. Principles
> of behavior analysis were used to teach, to control discipline, and
> to gain classroom efficiency. Results showed an increase in ex-
> perimental classes. Test formats, results, charts, and bibliography
> are appended.

Littky, Dennis, et al. SKILL ASSESSMENT AND INSTRUCTION PROGRAM.
New York: Institute for the Advancement of Urban Education, 1970. (ED 044
373)

> The authors describe a program developed for the Ocean Hill
> Brownsville School District to solve problems of teacher training,
> uses of community personnel, feedback, and accountability. The
> focus is on the teaching process. Curriculum development and
> assessment tools are treated. Uses of paraprofessionals are included.

Loretan, Joseph, and Umans, Shelley. TEACHING THE DISADVANTAGED.
New York: Columbia University, Teachers College Press, 1966.

> This book deals with the problem of the disadvantaged by recom-
> mending academic achievement rather than adjustment as the solu-
> tion to their problems. It insists that the disadvantaged have the
> capacity to achieve. It starts with a background of the concepts
> of the disadvantaged, then shows methods of teaching the various
> academic subjects. It does not include vocational education be-
> cause not all disadvantaged students should take vocational courses
> (as not all should have basic knowledge in academics).

Lusty, Beverly L., and Wood, Barbara Sundene. "Effects of an NDEA Institute
Upon Attitudes of Inner-City Elementary Teachers." SPEECH TEACHER 18 (September 1969): 217-22.

> Investigation within the area of teacher preparation reveals that
> most elementary teachers are inadequately trained to teach lan-
> guage, reading, composition, and speech. These findings have
> special significance for the quality of instruction provided for the
> inner-city child.

Lutonsky, Linda, ed. PORTAL SCHOOLS FINAL REPORT. Washington, D.C.:
Council of the Great City Schools, 1973. (ED 082 283)

> This monograph represents a collection of experiences of the initial
> developers of the Portal School strategy. This strategy brings sepa-
> rate educational institutions together into a working relationship to
> provide reality-based and field-centered teacher education as well
> as improved learning opportunities for children.

McCullough, Tom. "Urban Education, It's No Big Thing." URBAN EDUCA-
TION (July 1974): 117-35.

> The author discusses his experiences in a black inner-city school.
> Black children coming from home to attend school for the first time
> experience culture shock. The school environment is hostile. Teachers
> neither talk to each other nor help each other. The range of ob-
> servations on children and teachers is lengthy and informative. The
> author concludes questioning both whether a principal in an all-
> black school should be white, and the sources of black leadership.
> He provides subtle yet provocative questions to inner-city schools'
> questioning, among other topics, how they operate.

May, Angelita M. "Lock Haven's Inner-City Experiment Successful." PENN-
SYLVANIA EDUCATION 3 (March-April 1972): 32-35.

> This article describes the problems that student teachers encounter
> when entering the urban education field, and the ways that they
> are able to find to cope with these problems.

Neff, Franklin W., and Ahlstrom, Winton M. STUDENT OUTCOMES AND
STAFF ATTITUDES IN COMPENSATORY EDUCATION IN KANSAS CITY, MIS-
SOURI: A LIMITED EVALUATION OF PROGRAMS SUPPORTED BY TITLE I AND
MODEL CITIES. Kansas City, Mo.: Institute for Community Studies, 1973.
(ED 090 334)

> A division of Urban Education was established in 1966 with one of
> its major goals being improvement of instruction for inner-city chil-
> dren. Some of the things done to implement this decision were an
> expanded inservice training program for teachers, reading specialists
> assigned to some schools, and the introduction of the Sullivan Pro-
> grammed Reading program. Also included in the report is the way
> in which the basic study of program impact was to be done.

O'Brian, John L. PREPARING TO TEACH THE DISADVANTAGED. New York:
Free Press, 1969.

> This book represents an attempt to describe some of the characteris-
> tics of disadvantaged persons that affect their performance in an
> educational environment, potential causes of these characteristics,
> and the qualities of teachers and programs that are required to deal
> with these characteristics.

OPERATION PROBE: COOPERATIVE URBAN TEACHER EDUCATION. Kansas
City, Mo.: Mid-Continent Regional Educational Laboratory, 1968. (ED 028
965)

> This Urban Teacher Education program, a cooperative field experi-
> ence program for the recruitment and training of teachers for the
> inner city, is the focus for discussion of teacher education in this
> collection of speeches made at the Eighth National Clinic of the
> Association for Student Teaching.

Ornstein, Allan C. "Urban Teachers and Schools: Fashionable Targets." EDU-
CATIONAL FORUM 35 (March 1971): 359-66.

> Criticism of teachers who work among the poor is analyzed.

Ornstein, Allan C., and Vairo, Philip D. HOW TO TEACH DISADVANTAGED
YOUTH. New York: David McKay Co., 1969.

> This book points out the factors and forces that contribute to the
> unsuccessful attempts of ghetto school teachers, but also explores
> avenues open for successful and rewarding careers for teachers of
> disadvantaged youth. Lastly, it examines the role of teacher train-
> ing institutions in the preparation of teachers working with disad-
> vantaged youth.

Pedram, Manoychehr. "A Unique Approach to Inner City Teacher Education."
CLEARING HOUSE 45 (January 1971): 297-99.

"Poverty and the School." EDUCATIONAL LEADERSHIP 22 (May 1965): entire
issue.

> Mobility, motivation, self-concept, and education lag when poverty
> is present. Reeducation must start with the kindergarten child and
> continue on to the disadvantaged youth.

Proppe, William D. URBAN TEACHER TRAINING: A MULTI-AGENCY IDEN-
TIFICATION OF PROGRAM ELEMENTS AND ESTABLISHMENT OF CRITERIA FOR
DETERMINING CURRICULAR CONTENT. FINAL REPORT. Portland, Ore.:
Portland State University, School of Education, 1972. (ED 073 213)

> The purposes of this study were to: (1) design a system which would
> encourage participation of people from many sectors to produce sug-
> gestions on content and techniques which should be a part of urban
> education and teacher preparation, (2) establish criteria for selec-
> tion of curricular content for the training of urban teachers, and
> (3) identify some elements to be included in an urban teacher edu-
> cation and reeducation program.

Ralph, Ruth S. "General Semantics for Inner-City Teachers: A Summer Course."
ETC.: A REVIEW OF GENERAL SEMANTICS 31 (September 1974): 317-24.

> Ralph describes a summer-session workshop for inner-city teachers who
> wished to improve their professional performance or their teacher-
> student relationships.

READING INSERVICE PROGRAM. East Lansing: Michigan Education Association, 1972. (ED 071 055)

> The Michigan Education Association recommends a task-force ap-
> proach as one of the solutions to increasing the acquisition of ad-
> ditional communication skills for all elementary teachers. An in-
> service model was developed to be used primarily with inner-city

elementary pupils, but the basic design is applicable for use with any student group.

Rogers, Vincent R., and Weinland, Thomas P., eds. TEACHING SOCIAL STUDIES IN THE URBAN CLASSROOM. Reading, Mass.: Addison-Wesley Publishing Co., 1972. (ED 059 952)

This is a supplement for preservice and inservice courses for teach-ers of elementary social studies or urban education. It is designed to stimulate a positive and creative approach toward the teaching of social studies and to offer some specific examples. The articles represent grade levels four through twelve.

Schiff, Albert. THE PROBLEM OF RECRUITMENT. Brooklyn: New York City Board of Education, 1967. (ED 014 462)

This is a report of a program which begins the teacher selection process much earlier than the senior year of college. The person-nel division of the Detroit school system sponsors clubs of future teachers ranging from the elementary through the junior and senior high schools.

Schultheis, Robert. "Changing Business Teacher Education to Meet Inner-City Needs." NATIONAL BUSINESS EDUCATION QUARTERLY 38 (December 1969): 13-20.

Observing and tutoring, teaching, assisting a home-school coordina-tor, and working in a social agency are four methods for firsthand involvement with the problems of inner-city schools. Ten possible changes in business teacher education programs are presented and discussed.

Schwartz, Henrietta S. "An Experiment in Training Teachers for Inner-City Schools: A Social System's Approach in the Ford Training and Placement Program." Pa-per presented at the annual meeting of the American Educational Research Asso-ciation, Chicago, Illinois, April 1972. (ED 065 464)

This program, organized by the graduate department of the School of Education of the University of Chicago in cooperation with the Chicago Board of Education, trains and places new teachers in in-ner-city schools and retrains teachers in those schools. It empha-sizes a social system's approach to the training and placement of education professionals at various grade levels and in various sub-ject areas.

Smith, Calvert H. "Teaching in the Inner-City: Six Prerequisites to Success." TEACHER COLLEGE RECORD 73 (May 1972): 547-48.

This article discusses the importance of teacher attitudes and cul-tural orientation in successfully teaching in an inner-city community.

Smith, Lawrence C. "The Urban Studies Program." NASSP BULLETIN 54 (March 1970): 134-37.

This is a report on the program conducted in Washington, D.C.

Sobel, Max A., and Maletsky, Evan M. TEACHING MATHEMATICS TO THE SLOW LEARNER IN THE INNER-CITY SCHOOLS. Upper Montclair, N.J.: Montclair State College, 1972. (ED 076 515)

This was a 1972 Distinguished Achievement Award entry from Montclair State College. Twenty students participated in this three-week field experience program in which emphasis was placed on creative ways to motivate the slow learner through appropriate laboratory and experimental approaches. Recommendations were made for this program to be incorporated into the regular preservice mathematics curriculum.

Stewart, Marjorie S. "Interaction Between Social Agency Personnel and Home Economics Teachers." JOURNAL OF HOME ECONOMICS 63 (January 1971): 30-32.

The author of this article interviewed personnel from thirty-seven social agencies in Columbus, Ohio to determine how the social agencies could serve as resources for home economics teachers who have disadvantaged students. The results of her study indicate that social agency personnel are willing to help home economics teachers by complementing each other in the classroom as they try to improve the home and family lives of many of our youth.

Stone, James C. TEACHERS FOR THE DISADVANTAGED. San Francisco: Jossey-Bass, 1969.

This book contains the reports of the California project ESEA (Elementary Secondary Education Act) and the NDEA (National Defense Education Act) programs for the study of the disadvantaged.

Storen, Helen F. THE DISADVANTAGED EARLY ADOLESCENT: MORE EFFECTIVE TEACHING. New York: McGraw Hill, 1968.

This book contains a series of incidents and quotations from both students and teachers who participated in an inservice teacher training workshop sponsored by Queens College. Its purpose is to help teachers analyze their current teaching situation.

Symons, Mary Anne. "Foods Class Offers New Experiences for Disadvantaged." FORECAST FOR HOME ECONOMICS 14 (February 1969): 56-57.

The author feels that the teacher has a responsibility to identify the factors that contribute to making her students disadvantaged and that knowledge of foods can become an area of special interest which counteract some of these disadvantages. "It is a phase of home economics that offers much insight and help in dealing with the varying problems of poverty. As teachers, we must recognize the unique character of this subject area and capitalize on it."

Syropoulos, Mike. EVALUATION OF THE FEDERALLY ASSISTED STAFF TRAIN-
ING (FAST) PROJECT. Detroit: Detroit Public Schools, 1972. (ED 077 849)

> This project is designed for teachers in the inner-city schools. It
> covers the following phases: inservice consultant leadership train-
> ing, teacher behavior improvement workshops, and Title I staff train-
> ing in simulated and problem solving situations.

Taba, Hilda, and Elkins, Deborah. TEACHING STRATEGIES FOR THE CUL-
TURALLY DISADVANTAGED. Chicago: Rand McNally and Co., 1966.

> This book contains a series of curriculum, teaching, or learning se-
> quences. It deals with sixth, seventh, and eighth grade students
> that are deprived, and serves as a guide for programs to help teach
> these students.

Taxis, Linda A., ed. WHERE THE ACTION IS: SELECTED ADDRESSES AND
PROCEEDINGS OF THE AMERICAN INDUSTRIAL ARTS ASSOCIATION'S THIRTY-
FIRST ANNUAL CONVENTION AT LAS VEGAS. Washington, D.C.: American
Industrial Arts Association, 1969. (ED 038 544)

> Manuscripts of ninety-nine speeches are compiled under general sub-
> ject headings. The major topics are as follows: (1) curriculum de-
> velopment, (2) inner-city schools, (3) instructional systems, (4)
> teacher education, (5) vocational education, (6) information science,
> (7) elementary education, (8) special education, (9) supervision, and
> (10) power technology. A chronological index and a comprehensive
> subject and author index are included.

TEACHER CORPS: TWO YEARS OF PROGRESS AND PLANS FOR THE FUTURE.
Washington, D.C.: Teacher Corps, 1968. (ED 029 854)

> This interim report presents operational and evaluative concepts,
> results, and plans of the Teacher Corps from 1966 to 1968.

Tractenberg, Paul L. EQUAL EMPLOYMENT OPPORTUNITIES AND THE NEW
YORK CITY PUBLIC SCHOOLS: AN ANALYSIS AND RECOMMENDATIONS
BASED ON PUBLIC HEARINGS HELD JANUARY 25-29, 1971. New York: New
York City Commission on Human Rights, 1971. (ED 050 207)

> The essential issue raised by the hearings was whether the system
> that now prevails can be further modified to meet the divergent
> needs of all the individual schools and districts in the city, or
> whether more drastic change is required. The commission's investiga-
> tion of the current personnel practices of the New York City school
> system yields one inescapable conclusion--that change is urgently
> demanded.

Tuckman, Bruce W., and O'Brian, John L., eds. PREPARING TO TEACH THE
DISADVANTAGED: APPROACHES TO TEACHER EDUCATION. New York: Free
Press, 1969. (ED 029 006)

The book is divided into three sections to discuss the problems of teaching. Section 1 reviews the characteristics of the disadvantaged, sociological aspects of disadvantaged societies, and stigmatized youth and integration versus compensatory education. Section 2. describes programs for teaching, including vocational and practical experiences. Section 3 considers teacher-education programs. Recommendations for master degree programs to prepare effective empathic teachers through integration of practicums and interdisciplinary approaches are also included.

Walton, Joseph M. "An Instrument for Measuring Attitudes Toward Teaching In The Inner-City School." JOURNAL OF THE STUDENT PERSONNEL ASSOCIATION FOR TEACHER EDUCATION 13(June, 1975): 177-83. (Journal is now known as HUMANIST EDUCATOR.)

Walton presents an attitude scale designed to distinguish the prospective teacher with a positive attitude toward urban teaching from the teacher with a negative attitude.

Washington, Kenneth Ralph. AN ANALYSIS OF THE ATTITUDES OF PROSPECTIVE WHITE TEACHERS TOWARD THE INNER-CITY SCHOOLS. Boston: Boston College, School of Education, 1968. (ED 083 176)

Two studies were done on the attitudes of prospective white teachers toward inner-city schools. The first study, using Osgood's Semantic Differential, investigated whether 250 prospective white teachers from a major teacher training institution held more positive attitudes toward suburban or inner-city schools. The second study investigated whether a positive shift in the attitudes of prospective white teachers would be evident following exposure to inner-city schools.

Webster, Staten W. THE DISADVANTAGED LEARNER. VOL. 3: EDUCATING THE DISADVANTAGED LEARNER. San Francisco: Chandler Publishing Co., 1966.

This volume contains articles by a number of authorities pertaining primarily to problems found in the education of the disadvantaged, suggesting guidelines to follow in dealing with such problems. They also discuss methods and ways of presenting material to the students.

_____. THE DISADVANTAGED LEARNER. VOL. 1: KNOWING THE DISADVANTAGED. San Francisco: Chandler Publishing Co., 1966.

This collection of writings seeks to familiarize the reader with the various disadvantaged groups in this country, aiming to increase the reader's awareness and understanding of problems associated with teaching disadvantaged students. Also some of the approaches used by educators in attempting to more effectively educate the disadvantaged are introduced.

Weinswig, S. Edward, and Freedman, Albert I. HICUT '68: DESIGN FOR DE-
VELOPMENT. Hartford, Conn.: Hartford Public Schools, 1968. (ED 024 660)

> This report of the Hartford Intensive City-University Teacher Train-
> ing Project (HICUT) is a projection of the 1968 program, based upon
> the 1967 program. Included is background information describing
> HICUT and its objective.

Winer, Ronald M. "The Crucial Factor in Urban Education: An Intensive Teacher-
To-Teacher Training Program for Urban Schools." JOURNAL OF TEACHER EDU-
CATION 21 (Summer 1970): 240-43.

> The author addresses the critical problem of the urban schools' in-
> ability to meet their obligations in the transmission of equal oppor-
> tunity in education. Teacher training for the urban school is fo-
> cused upon as a key component which, if properly developed, will
> assist in meeting the problems with an adequate solution. Teacher
> training, it is proposed, should be considered in the total perspec-
> tive of the school rather than simply as a separate issue.

Winn, Ulysses Richard. "An Assessment of How Inservice Recipients, Inservice
Instructors and Decision-Makers Perceive a Teacher Training Inservice Program
in a Model Neighborhood Area." Ph.D. dissertation, University of Pittsburgh,
1974.

> This study provides an evaluation of the Center for Educational Ac-
> tion's (CEA's) Teacher Training Inservice Program for educational
> personnel within a Model Neighborhood Area (MNA). The overall
> effectiveness of the program is outlined and analyzed. The com-
> ment of the author relative to this evaluation was that all the prom-
> ises made by the program were not carried through. This was af-
> fected by the variables of (1) time, (2) future funding, (3) orien-
> tation, and (4) communication patterns.

Yanofsky, Saul M. UPDATE ON PAS: A LOOK AT THE ADVANCEMENT
SCHOOL'S ACTIVITIES SINCE ITS ESTABLISHMENT IN PHILADELPHIA, SEPTEM-
BER, 1967 TO DECEMBER, 1970. Philadelphia: Pennsylvania Advancement
School, 1971. (ED 048 399)

> In this paper, general information about the school's activities is
> presented. The paper is divided into three sections: (1) activities
> that constitute PAS's core program, (2) staff development and con-
> sultant services related to the core program, and (3) other activi-
> ties in which the school or individual staff members participated.

Zondlak, Allen Frank. "Perceptions of the Role of the Curricular Leader in
Model Neighborhood Elementary Schools of Detroit." Ed.D. dissertation, Wayne
State University, 1971.

> The variables studied in this work were (1) bureaucratized profes-
> sionalism, (2) the relationship of professionals to their clients, and
> (3) school decentralization. The hypothesis concerned the predic-
> tion of the principal's attitude toward decentralization as indicated

by his assessment of his pedagogical staff. The hypothesis was not supported in this study but the bases for further study are outlined in-depth.

Section D

COMMUNITY CONTROL

Abraham, Cleo. "Protests and Expedients in Response to Failures in Urban Education: A Study of New Haven." Ed.D. dissertation, University of Massachusetts, 1971.

> This study examines the impact of the public school system's failures with minority students. The response of inner-city residents is considered to have been one of increasing activism. This study examines socioeconomic and other data over a twenty-year period.

Alverson, Hoyt S., and Cohen, Lucy M. "Community Researchers Meet Community Residents; Interpretation of the Findings." COMMUNITY PARTICIPATION 32 (Fall 1973): 243-45.

> This article concerns itself with the ability of researchers to be responsive to their peers and to the community in which research is done.

Amez, Nancy L. PARTNERS IN URBAN EDUCATION; TEACHING THE INNER CITY CHILD. Morristown, N.J.: Silver Burdett General Learning Corp., 1973.

> This book focuses on the myriad of facts, ideas, and explanations for the roles of parents and teachers in inner-city schools. The author discusses the utilization of community resources in bringing effectiveness to schools.

Bauer, Raymond, et al. URBAN EDUCATION: EIGHT EXPERIMENTS IN COMMUNITY CONTROL. Cambridge, Mass.: Arthur D. Little, 1969.

> One principal hypothesis which suggests a means for breaking the poverty cycle is to make school systems responsive to particular educational needs of the socially and economically disadvantaged. This report isolates four models of change presently being discussed or experimented with in attempting to change this pattern: local community control, total community involvement, setting up a competitive system as found in American business, and changing present board behavior.

Blanchard, Walter J. INNER CITY PROVIDENCE: IMPLICATIONS FOR EDU-
CATION. ATTACHMENT 2. Providence: Providence Public Schools and Rhode
Island College, 1967. (ED 048 063)

> This is a collection of raw data and brief descriptions of the neighbor-
> hoods of Providence, Rhode Island for use by teachers, staff, and
> community leaders in program planning.

Briggs, Albert A. "Educational Decision-Making." NASSP BULLETIN 53 (May
1969): 176-80.

> This paper was presented at the annual convention of the National
> Association of Secondary School Principals (53rd, San Francisco,
> California, 28 February-5 March 1969).

Broadbelt, Samuel. "The Plight of the Cities and Citizen Commitment." EDU-
CATION AND URBAN SOCIETY 3 (May 1971): 265-76.

> Because of urban problems, public education is presently undergo-
> ing its greatest challenge in the cities. Citizens of the nation
> have the technical skills to solve problems, but presently lack the
> moral commitment necessary.

Brown, Roscoe C., Jr. "How to Make Educational Research Relevant to the
Urban Community--The Researcher's View." Paper presented at the annual meeting of the American Educational Research Association, New York, New York,
5 February 1971. (ED 049 347)

> This paper suggests that "residents of the urban community are not
> antiresearch. When the purposes and scope of the research are ex-
> plained to them carefully and when they are given some opportun-
> ity to be involved in the conceptualization, data collection, and
> interpretation of research, they will support educational research
> enthusiastically."

Coulson, William R. "Community Lies Beyond Detachment, Beyond Advocacy."
NATIONAL CATHOLIC GUIDANCE CONFERENCE JOURNAL 15 (Fall 1970):
11-16.

> This article stresses the need for school-community discussion groups as
> an alternative to violence, particularly in ghetto areas. This con-
> cept demands vulnerability from each participant for full group com-
> munication.

Criscuolo, Nicholas P. "Meaningful Parental Involvement in the Reading Program." NATIONAL ELEMENTARY PRINCIPAL 51 (April 1972): 64-65.

_____. "Six Successful Reading Programs for Inner City Schools." CHILD-
HOOD EDUCATION 47 (April 1971): 371-72.

The author emphasizes the need for a strong partnership between community and school in developing successful reading programs for inner-city children.

Dolan, Jeanne, and Parsons, Tim. A NEW CONSCIOUSNESS: CHALLENGING, CHOOSING, CHANGING. THE STORY OF THE IRONBOUND COMMUNITY LEARNING CENTER. Perspective Series No. 6. Trenton, N.J.: State Department of Education, Division of Research, Planning and Evaluation, 1974. (ED 097 763)

The publication describes a Newark, New Jersey community learning center composed of three programs: (1) a day-care center, (2) an after-school and summer program, and (3) a community school (K through 8). Parent decision making, staff-parent communication, and open education are stressed.

Falkson, Joseph L., and Grainer, Marc A. "Neighborhood School Politics and Constituency Organizations." SCHOOL REVIEW 81 (November 1972): 35-61.

The authors study the major factors as the core of school-community political relationships.

Fantini, Mario D. "Participation, Decentralization and Community Control." NATIONAL ELEMENTARY PRINCIPAL 48 (April 1969): 25-31.

_____. "Participation, Decentralization, Community Control and Quality Education." TEACHERS COLLEGE RECORD 71 (September 1969): 93-107.

Feld, Marcia Sandra Marker. "Citizen Participation in Urban Education Planning: The Consultation Process." Ph.D. dissertation, Harvard University, 1973.

A FINAL PROGRAM REPORT FROM THE UNIVERSITY OF ILLINOIS, CHICAGO CIRCLE AND THE CHICAGO PUBLIC SCHOOLS, 1971-74. Chicago: Chicago Board of Education and Illinois University, 1974. (ED 116-097)

The University of Illinois at Chicago Circle's College of Education and the Department of Educational Psychology at the Urbana campus are working in conjunction with Chicago School District #9 and the Midwest Center at Indiana University to develop and test a model aimed at improving the educational atmosphere of a large inner-city high school.

Finkelstein, Leonard B., and Strick, Lisa W. "Learning in the City." PROSPECTS 2 (Spring 1972): 72-76.

Gross, Mary J., et al. COMBINED HUMAN EFFORTS IN ELEVATING ACHIEVEMENT AT THE WHEATLEY SCHOOL, Washington, D.C. Ed.D. practicum, Nova University, 1974. (ED 102 666)

Planning and implementing a comprehensive development program for the staff, parents, and community at an inner-city elementary school was the purpose of this practicum. The school served a disadvantaged, segregated student population.

Hanusey, Richard Dmytro. "A Study of the Influences of Neighborhood Association on Public Schools of an Urban District as Perceived by Administrators." Ed.D. dissertation, Temple University, 1973.

This study attempts to examine the influences of neighborhood associations on an urban public school system. The study outlines the perceptions of administrators. These appeared to form the basis for priorities in educational concerns. The study produced a set of recommendations for improving relations between administrators and neighborhood associations.

Holliday, Frederick Douglas. "The Improvement of a Program of Cyesis Education at Gratz Neighborhood High (Philadelphia) in Conjunction with an Unstructured Community Advisory Board." Ph.D. dissertation, Harvard University, 1970.

Howell, Barbara Thompson. PARTNERS IN URBAN EDUCATION: GETTING IT TOGETHER AT HOME. Morristown, N.J.: General Learning Corp., 1972. (ED 104 993)

This handbook, written for the parents of a school-age child, is organized into an introduction and five chapters. The purpose of the handbook is to help parents get their child a good education by providing ideas about working with the child, with his teachers, and with other parents, as well as using the home and community to help the child learn.

Jackson, Kathleen O'Brien, comp. ANNOTATED BIBLIOGRAPHY ON SCHOOL COMMUNITY RELATIONS. Eugene: ERIC Clearinghouse on Educational Administration, University of Oregon, 1969. (ED 030 220)

This bibliography is divided into four categories: general discussion, school politics and community power structure, schools and public relations, and schools and urban relations.

Jameson, Irene Suflas. "A Study of the Intended Influences of Neighborhood Associations on the Public Schools of an Urban School District." Ed.D. dissertation, Temple University, 1973.

This study attempts to investigate the influences of neighborhood associations on an urban public school system and to develop and recommend guidelines to improve relationships between these groups. There is strong concern over the patterns of communications that effect the ability to influence as well as conflict over bases for evaluations made by the respective groups. The instance of crisis oriented organizational planning appears to be commonplace. The study provides conclusions and recommendations.

Jameson, Spenser, and Ianni, Frances A. THE READING PROCESS AND PRO-
CESSED READING. Washington, D.C.: Academy for Educational Development,
1970. (ED 039 737)

> It is imperative for a successful program of technological develop-
> ment in urban education to understand the psychocultural system of
> the ghetto and to develop both software and hardware out of an
> understanding of this system, rather than to impose existing devices
> and techniques on it. In community-based "learning centers," all
> members of the community--people living, studying, teaching, or
> marketing--would have the opportunity to become involved in the
> solution of education problems.

Janowitz, Morris. INSTITUTIONAL BUILDING IN URBAN EDUCATION. New
York: Russell Sage Foundation, 1969. (ED 041 959)

> This book presents a sociological perspective on the issues involved
> in transforming the institutional structure of inner-city schools, and
> discusses the closing of the gap between sociological analysis and
> policy, and professional practice of citizen participation.

Kealey, Robert J. "Why Do Catholic Black and Hispanic Women Support Catholic Schools?" NOTRE DAME JOURNAL OF EDUCATION 6 (Spring 1975):
32-35.

> Today, mainly black and Hispanic children are enrolled in inner-
> city Catholic elementary schools. This study was made to deter-
> mine the reasons black and Hispanic female parish leaders in par-
> ticular are supporting Catholic education.

Kelley, James A. "Priorities in Urban Education." Paper presented at the Conference on a National Agenda for American Education, Washington, D.C., 17
July 1969. (ED 033 461)

> The disparities between urban and nonurban education can be changed
> through community participation and a redistribution of educational
> revenues. The high positive correlation of race and economic class
> to school achievement is the most pressing concern of education to-
> day. Public pressure is necessary to resist the tendency toward bu-
> reaucratic isolation of school systems and to force school officials
> to be more accountable for their product in terms of pupil achieve-
> ment.

Kleinfeld, Judith. "'Sense of Fate Control' and Community Control of the
Schools." EDUCATION AND URBAN SOCIETY 3 (May 1971): 277-300.

> Kleinfeld examines the nature of the "sense of fate control" find-
> ings of the Coleman Report, and argues that these findings are ir-
> relevant to the debate over community control.

Lusthaus, Evelyn W., et al. "Influencing Patterns of Emerging Education Interest Groups in Urban Communities." Paper presented at the annual meeting of the American Educational Research Association, Washington, D.C., April 1975. (ED 105 036)

A systems model is employed here to illustrate, categorize, and explore the dynamics of the political patterns of interaction. The model is utilized to interpret data obtained from three CEIGs (community education interest groups) operating in a large northeastern city.

Masters, Nicholas A. POLITICS, POVERTY AND EDUCATION: AN ANALYSIS OF DECISION-MAKING STRUCTURES. University Park: Pennsylvania State University, 1968.

The purpose of the research was to examine the interrelationship of community action agencies and school systems in six urban centers throughout the United States.

May, Lucius J. "Community Involvement: The Detroit Experience." COMMUNITY EDUCATION JOURNAL 3 (May-June 1974): 52-53.

This article relates some of the significant developments arising from one large school district's quest for meaningful school-community involvement.

Mesa, Pete. COMMUNITY INVOLVEMENT AND INSERVICE TEACHER EDUCATION: THE URBAN/RURAL APPROACH. Washington, D.C.: ERIC Clearinghouse on Teacher Education, 1976. (ED 117 034)

This paper describes the history and status of the Urban-Rural School Development Program which has both community involvement and inservice teacher education as components.

Mills, Nicolaus. "Community Schools: Irish, Italians, and Jews." SOCIETY 11 (March-April 1974): 76-84.

Mills examines the scope and variety of past demands for community-controlled schools in New York, which were especially visible in the actions of three groups: Irish Catholics in the 1840s, Jews in the period surrounding the turn of the century, and Italians in the middle 1930s and early 1940s.

_____. SCHOOLS AND THE DISADVANTAGED: A STUDY IN POLITICAL STRATEGY. New York: Columbia University, ERIC Clearinghouse on the Urban Disadvantaged, 1971. (ED 054 269)

This essay focuses on the politics of public education for the disadvantaged. Specifically, an attempt is made to describe the conditions under which the disadvantaged have sought to change the public schools by adopting one of two political strategies--integration or community control.

Mullarney, Patrick. "Boston Mayor, Kevin H. White Discusses Community

Schools and Their Importance to Urban Socio-Political Life." COMMUNITY
EDUCATION JOURNAL 4 (September-October 1974): 31-33, 61.

This article is a question-and-answer consideration of community
schools and the governance of them. The concept of community
schools is discussed as well as the reasons for the adoption of this
concept. The Boston approach includes the administration of community schools by the Department of Public Facilities rather than
the Department of Public Schools. The interview covers a full
range of inquiries and the responses are tied to the Boston experiences.

Ornstein, Allan C.; Levine, Daniel U.; and Wilkerson, Doxey A. REFORMING
METROPOLITAN SCHOOLS. Pacific Palisades, Calif.: Goodyear, 1974.

This book gives an in-depth look at urban education with particular
focus on compensatory education. Other issues covered are desegregation, community control of schools, and accountability.

Oscarson, Janice M. "Community Involvement in Accountability." JOURNAL
OF RESEARCH AND DEVELOPMENT IN EDUCATION 5 (Fall 1971): 79-86.

Interim evaluations of the Indianapolis Model Cities School Program
point in positive directions in pupil performance and self concept.

O'Shea, David. "Theoretical Perspectives on Social District Decentralization."
Paper presented at the annual meeting of the American Educational Research Association, Chicago, Illinois, April 1974. (ED 094 028)

Drawing largely on data from Los Angeles, but with reference to
other cities where appropriate, this paper attempts to clarify the
distinctive positions taken by advocates of community control as
opposed to proponents of administrative decentralization.

Peel, Mark Steven. "A Reform Strategy in Urban Education: Community Action." Ed.D. dissertation, University of Massachusetts, 1973.

The subject of institutional change is studied in this article through
the background and development of the New Haven Community Action Coalition. The identified changes were the shifting of leadership roles, the decentralization of organizational structures, and the
pluralization of decision making procedures. These processes are
noted to have occurred within the school system, but also within the
community service structure.

Phillips, W. M., Jr., et al. PARTICIPATION OF THE BLACK COMMUNITY
IN SELECTED ASPECTS OF THE EDUCATIONAL INSTITUTION OF
NEWARK, 1958-1972. FINAL REPORT. New Brunswick, N.J.: Rutgers, The
State University, 1973.

This document is the final report of a two-year study of the inter-
dependency of race and education in Newark, New Jersey. The

report is organized into sections describing how the research was performed and presents the results on a set of topics defined as central for providing a useful understanding of the complex inter-relationships of race and education.

Poidevin, William, et al. STUDENT PERSONNEL: PROJECT DESIGN, EDU-CATIONAL NEEDS. Fresno, Calif.: Fresno City Unified School District, 1968. (ED 038 761)

The purpose of this study was to determine if the students in the district have the opportunity to be involved in a developmental, comprehensive, cocurricular program.

Polley, John W., and Lamitie, Robert E. IMPROVING PROVISIONS FOR ORGANIZATION, HOUSING, FINANCIAL SUPPORT AND ACCOUNTABILITY. Denver: Colorado State Department of Education, 1972. (ED 065 918)

Chapter 4 provides insights into the solution of financial and gov-ernance problems that face big-city education. The report identi-fies recent developments affecting big-city education such as me-tropolitanism, regionalism, full state financing, revenue sharing, and reform of property taxation.

Pope, Lillie. "Blueprint for a Successful Paraprofessional Tutorial Program." Paper presented at the meeting of the American Orthopsychiatric Association, San Francisco, California, 25 March 1970. (ED 043 463)

The use of paraprofessionals as tutors for retarded readers has proved successful in reducing the number of school failures. Described here is a program that uses paraprofessionals drawn from the school's neighborhood in order to involve the community in solving some of its problems.

Ravitz, Mel. URBAN EDUCATION: TODAY AND TOMORROW. Detroit: Wayne State University, 1970. (ED 040 227)

If needed, significant educational change is to be achieved, some countervailing power source capable of confronting administrative bureaucracy and making it conform to the present needs of the public must be established. Community control, the subdivision of the large system into appropriate communities, and the control of each community by its local citizens and their appointees, mer-its a trial.

Riley, William Wayne. "Neighborhood School Boards: A Study of Decentrali-zation of Decision Making." Ph.D. dissertation, Southern Illinois University, 1973.

The investigation and discussion of neighborhood school boards fo-cuses on composition and function of members, and its function as a group. The ability of this structure to provide an alternative

in planning for decentralization of schools is documented in the
Louisville, Kentucky experience.

Roger, Harrel R. COMMUNITY CONFLICT, PUBLIC OPINION AND THE
LAW, OPINION AND THE LAW, THE AMISH. Columbus, Ohio: Charles
E. Merrill Publishing Co., 1968 .

This book has a community-control thesis concerning variables of
community conflict and public opinion.

Rubinstein, Annette T. SCHOOLS AGAINST CHILDREN (THE CASE FOR
COMMUNITY CONTROL). New York: Monthly Review Press, 1970.

This consists of compiled studies by experts as to the potential for
community control of schools to further help the disadvantaged child.

Schwartz, Richard. PROJECT UNIQUE. A REPORT. New York: Center for
Urban Education, Program Reference Service, 1971. (ED 055 127)

This project, developed by the Rochester public school system,
sought to do the following: (1) increase community participation
of inner-city parents in the educational process, (2) recruit black
and Spanish-speaking teachers, (3) improve the racial balance of
urban and suburban schools, (4) produce a "working partnership"
with the business community, and (5) develop new modes of instruction.

Sciara, Frank J., and Jantz, Richard K. A REPORT OF THE EVALUATION
OF THE EFFECTIVENESS OF TEACHER AIDES IN INDIANAPOLIS MODEL
CITIES SCHOOLS. Indianapolis: Indianapolis Public Schools, 1972.

The effectiveness of teacher aides in eight Indianapolis Model
Cities Schools as perceived by themselves and others is the concern of this study. These paraprofessional personnel were hired
to provide additional help to teachers and children in the classroom, and to provide career opportunities for some of the indigenous residents from the school attendance areas.

Scott, Robert, et al. URBAN SCHOOL DECENTRALIZATION. NATIONAL
ISSUES AND PROSPECTS FOR SAN FRANCISCO. San Francisco: San Francisco Center for Public Education, 1974. (ED 121 873)

This publication covers background and issues, specific decentralization experiments including decentralization in San Francisco.
An overall summary is presented of the interviews with community
representatives and members of the board of education involved in
voting on proposals to formally decentralize the school district.
Also included are sources of information on and brief descriptions
of decentralization structures in five cities not discussed in the
text.

Shade, Barbara J. URBAN EDUCATION AND THE STATE EDUCATIONAL
AGENCY: A PROPOSAL FOR EDUCATIONAL CHANGE. Madison: Wisconsin State Department of Public Instruction, 1974. (ED 103 512)

> This author suggests a model for establishing more community con-
> trol through the use of a superintendent's council and an urban
> education advisory committee.

Sherry, Len T. THE CURRICULUM SYSTEM OPERATING IN URBAN SCHOOLS.
Springfield: Illinois State Commission on Urban Education, 1970. (ED 044 453)

> This paper presents a contextual statement from which to consider
> contemporary educational problems. The operations of the curricu-
> lum system in an urban environment are surveyed. The three pri-
> mary functions of the system, production, implementation, and
> evaluation, have been described in depth. It is suggested that
> issues such as decentralization, control, relevance of content, and
> improved instruction are basically curriculum questions with inter-
> related functions which have effects upon the total curriculum sys-
> tem.

Silcott, T. George. "Child Care Model for Urban Communities." Paper presented at the 50th annual meeting of the American Orthopsychiatric Association, New York, New York, May 1973. (ED 089 845)

> The development, for inner-city ghetto youth, of a child-care
> model that functions within a family-neighborhood framework rather
> than from the "safety" of distant residential treatment centers, is
> essential to the goal of eliminating the fragmentation and inade-
> quacy of such services, and the continued disregard of the prerog-
> atives and rights of ghetto parents and children.

Silverman, William, ed. "Legal Developments in Urban Education." EDUCA-
TION AND URBAN SOCIETY 3 (May 1971): 373-78.

> Amish parents who refused to enroll their children in high school
> (because of religious tenets) violated the Wisconsin Compulsory
> School Attendance Law. The court ruled the law unconstitutional
> as it applied to these parents, opening issues for current commun-
> ity control.

SIMU-SCHOOL: CENTER FOR URBAN EDUCATIONAL PLANNING. Chicago:
Chicago Board of Education, 1973. (ED 082 284)

> Simu-School is intended to provide the action-oriented organiza-
> tional and functional framework necessary for tackling the problems
> of modern-day education planning.

Singh, P. "City Center Schools and Community Relations." TRENDS IN EDU-
CATION 33 (May 1974): 27-30.

Children's racial attitudes are beginning to be formed long before they go to school. What can city-center schools do to ease racial tension?

Smith, Mortimer. "The Failure of 'Community Control.'" COMPACT 3 (April 1969): 14-15.

Summerfield, Harry Louis. "The Neighborhood-Based Politics of Education in the Central City: An Analysis of Education Politics in Four Socio-Economically Differentiated Central City Neighborhoods." Ph.D. dissertation, University of Minnesota, 1969.

The systematic inquiry into neighborhood politics is studied. The factors considered are economically differentiated neighborhoods. The findings suggest that the characteristics of a neighborhood are determined primarily by the problems confronting it and the availability of resources from which it can draw upon. The analysis organized the facts into four vignettes which outline the major findings.

Toffler, Alvin, ed. THE SCHOOLHOUSE IN THE CITY. New York: Frederick A. Praeger, 1968.

A conference entitled "The Schoolhouse in the City" was convened at Stanford University, 10-14 July 1967, and sponsored by Stanford's School Planning Laboratory and supported by Educational Facilities Laboratories and the Office of Education. The conference brought together as speakers leading figures in local, state, and federal government, civil rights, sociology, psychology, and urban planning as well as education and architecture.

Tyack, David B. THE ONE BEST SYSTEM: A HISTORY OF AMERICAN URBAN EDUCATION. Cambridge, Mass.: Harvard University Press, 1974.

This book concentrates on the years from 1870 to 1930. The themes range from conflicts over centralization of schools, school boards, the rise of experts in administration, the role of experimental psychology, the development of testing and tracking, the plight of blacks in segregated schools, and the persuasive ethnocentrism in the American educational ideology.

WAYS OF ESTABLISHING AND FUNDING COMMUNITY LEARNING CENTERS, FINAL REPORT. New York: Center for Urban Education, 1971. (ED 091 480)

There are three sections of this report on projects designed to increase citizen participation in urban education. The sections are: citizen participation, social education, and evaluation.

Wayson, William W. "Educating for Renewal in Urban Communities." NA-
TIONAL ELEMENTARY PRINCIPAL 51 (April 1972): 6-18.

> Urban education needs can be met if principals accept leadership
> responsibility and promote school-community involvement.

Wheeler, Calvin Coolidge. "A Case Study of Responses to an Urban Education
Facilities Planning Charrette in Des Moines, Iowa." Ph.D. dissertation, Michigan State University, 1973.

> The evaluation of the charrette process, a method of involving
> school community in facilities planning, is the topic of this thesis.
> The author gives a lengthy discussion of the data gathered in this
> case study. The ability to include groups in facility planning is
> concluded to have beneficial impact.

Wilder, David E., et al. ACTUAL AND PERCEIVED CONCENSUS ON EDU-
CATIONAL GOALS BETWEEN SCHOOL AND COMMUNITY. FINAL REPORT.
New York: Columbia University, Bureau of Applied Research, 1968. (ED 023
939)

> Based on interview response data collected in 1965 in representa-
> tive New Jersey communities, this social-integration study sought
> to determine the extent of consensus regarding educational goals
> as perceived by parents, teachers, and students. Copies of survey
> instruments are appended.

Winkelstein, Ellen. "A Community-University Model for Urban Preschool Education." Paper presented at the annual meeting of the American Educational
Research Association, New York, New York, 4 February 1971. (ED 047 373)

> The objective of the model was to provide the means for an urban
> community to operate a preschool program. The community made
> ultimate program decisions, the community and the university ad-
> ministered program decisions and planned curriculum, and the uni-
> versity provided a training program for students and parents.

Winston, Eric V.A., comp. DIRECTORY OF URBAN AFFAIRS INFORMATION
AND RESEARCH CENTERS. Metuchen, N.J.: Scarecrow Press, 1970. (ED
047 066)

> This directory of urban affairs information and research centers seeks
> to bring to the attention of urban researchers those organizations,
> agencies, and institutions which are actively involved in the erad-
> ication of current urban ills.

Yin, Robert K., et al. CITIZEN ORGANIZATIONS: INCREASING CLIENT
CONTROL OVER SERVICES. Washington, D.C.: RAND Corp., 1973.

> This report attempts to identify the forms and characteristics of cit-
> izen participation that facilitate the effective exertion of citizen

power over program administration. The objectives of the study were to review prior experience and research concerning various forms of citizen participation, and to derive from them information that would assist the Department of Health, Education, and Welfare in drafting guidelines and model bylaws for citizen participation in specific DHEW programs.

Section E

PROSPECTS OF URBAN EDUCATION

Allen, Anita F. "Perspectives on Quality Education." EDUCATIONAL HORI-ZONS 49 (Summer 1971): 100-107.

Allen, James E., Jr. "Non-Urban School Boards and the Problem of Urban Education." Remarks before the 48th annual convention of the New York State Boards Association, Syracuse, New York, 23 October 1967. (ED 035 076)

> The author's position is that an effective attack on the problems of urban education in New York must come from all school board members, regardless of their location in the state.

_____. "Urban Education Crisis: The Need for Agreement on Procedure." Speech presented at the National Council of Urban Education Associations meeting, Philadelphia, Pennsylvania, 27 June 1969. (ED 032 374)

> This speech by the U.S. Commissioner of Education discusses the urgency of finding solutions to problems of urban education. He states that the most important issues to be faced are the metropolitanization of the country and the anticipated high birthrate within the major population centers. Increasing too are the demands for better service from all governmental units. Solutions to these challenges must involve consensus on procedures and programs for achieving quality urban education.

Alloway, David N., and Cordasco, Francesco. MINORITIES AND THE AMERI-CAN CITY: A SOCIOLOGICAL PRIMER FOR EDUCATORS. New York: David McKay Co., 1970. (ED 044 459)

> This monograph attempts to set the new minorities of American cities with a historically intelligible context and seeks to clarify the complexity as well as the origin of urban problems.

Barney, William J., Jr. "Poverty and Education: Some Observation." CONNECTICUT TEACHER 38 (March 1971): 15-17.

> Sixteen million children of poverty are fed into the school system

and face a hopeless future. Among their problems are lack of pride and identity, no sense of being, no reason to desire an education, and no sense of belonging. The schools and society should develop a commitment to alleviating these problems.

Booms, Bernard. "Economic and Social Factors in the Provision of Urban Public Education." AMERICAN JOURNAL OF ECONOMICS AND SOCIOLOGY 32 (January 1973): 35-43.

Booms attempts to explore the fiscal relationships underlying the provision of elementary and secondary public education by introducing a simultaneous equation model. The model is essentially a demand-and-supply equation system for public expenditures on education. It represents a preliminary attempt at providing predictive insight and understanding for the determinants of community public education investment decisions.

Bottomly, Forbes. "The Foreseeable Future of Metropolitan School Organization." THRUST 3 (May 1974): 19-21.

The author discusses the development and growth of educational collaboratives to deal with problems in the larger city school districts.

Callahan, John J., and Wilken, William H. "School Finance Reform in the States: What Should Be Done?" Paper presented at the annual meeting of the National Educational Finance Project, Atlanta, Georgia, 2 April 1973. (ED 079 865)

This document examines the effect that alternative ways of reforming school finance would have on major city school districts.

Chisholm, Shirley. "Educational Challenges." Paper presented at the annual convention of the American Association of School Administrators, Atlantic City, New Jersey, 20 February 1976. (ED 117 856)

The author identifies three important factors that contribute substantially to urban fiscal problems in providing educational services.

Clark, Kenneth B. "Educational Stimulation of Racially Disadvantaged Children." In EDUCATION IN DEPRESSED AREAS, edited by Harry Passow, pp. 142-62. New York: Teachers College Press, 1966.

This book stresses that the fundamental task of school in stimulating academic achievement in disadvantaged children is to provide the conditions necessary for building self-image. Believing in integration and the importance of having the opportunity to feel successful and the use of materials suited to those needs is discussed. The author disagrees with James B. Conant's view in "Slums and Suburbs."

Clasby, Miriam. "Education for Changing: A Case Study of Hawthorne House as an Urban Education Center." Ed.D. dissertation, Harvard University, 1971.

This work provides the procedures to organize and analyze information and experience in planning an educational system, and also examines the social function of the system. The results are the linkage of the experiential reality to educational theory.

Clothier, Grant M., and Hudgins, Bryce B. UNIQUE CHALLENGES OF PREPARING TEACHERS FOR INNER-CITY SCHOOLS: PROGRESS AND PROSPECTS. Kansas City, Mo.: Mid-Continent Regional Educational Laboratory, 1971. (ED 056 971)

For annotation see section D, Clothier, Grant M.

Cordasco, Francesco. "The Urban Demos and the School." EDUCATIONAL FORUM 40 (January 1976): 179-84.

This article examines the problems of urban education.

Cunningham, Luvern L. "Educational Governance and Policy Making in Large Cities." PUBLIC ADMINISTRATION REVIEW 30 (July-August 1970): 333-39.

Davidson, Helen H., and Lang, Gerhard. "Children's Perceptions of Their Teachers' Feelings Toward Them Related to Self-Perception, School Achievement, and Behavior." JOURNAL OF EXPERIMENTAL EDUCATION 20 (December 1960): 107-18.

A teacher is a significant person in the life of every student. The authors present and discuss research findings related to the impact of the teacher on various aspects of development for children of all social classes.

Dentler, Robert A. "Innovations in Public Education in New York City." CITY ALMANAC 6 (December 1971): 1-9. (ED 059 324)

Five major themes mark the development of public education in New York City from its early nineteenth century beginning to the mid-twentieth century: (1) the effort to provide free education for all children through the twelfth grade, (2) the development of special schools and programs for gifted youth, (3) the development of programs for children with special difficulties, (4) the elaboration of a highly-standardized grade structure, curriculum, and procedures for the mass of children, and (5) a contrasting theme of experimentation and innovation.

Dror, Yehezkel. URBAN METAPOLICY AND URBAN EDUCATION. Santa Monica, Calif.: RAND Corp., 1970. (ED 051 343)

The main thesis of this paper is that innovative changes in both urban metapolicy and in urban education are needed to meet present and future urban problems. Metapolicy deals with policies on policymaking, including the characteristics of the policymaking system, and basic policy frameworks and postures.

Eckstein, Max A. "Schooling in the Metropolis: A Comparative View." TEACHERS COLLEGE RECORD 73 (May 1972): 507-18.

This article describes educational problems inherent in the modern metropolis.

Eckstein, Max A., and Noah, Harold J. METROPOLITANISM AND EDUCATION: TEACHERS AND SCHOOLS IN AMSTERDAM, LONDON, PARIS AND NEW YORK. New York: Columbia University, Institute of Philosophy and Politics of Education, 1973.

The twin rationales for this study are: (1) that the educational implications of metropolitan conditions deserve further study, and (2) that these implications transcend national boundaries.

EDUCATION AND MANPOWER STRATEGIES AND PROGRAMS FOR DEPRIVED URBAN NEIGHBORHOODS: THE MODEL CITIES APPROACH. FINAL REPORT. Washington, D.C.: National League of Cities, 1968. (ED 025 629)

This report attempts to identify effective strategies that might be used by city and school administrators in planning, initiating, and coordinating comprehensive, deprived neighborhood manpower and education programs.

Fadiman, Clifton, ed. "What Are The Priorities for City Schools? A Discussion by Wilson C. Riles, Carl J. Dolce, and Martin Mayer. Occasional Papers No. 15." Discussion at a public meeting of the Council for Basic Education, Washington, D.C., 25 October 1968. (ED 096 382)

Many of the problems the schools seem to face are problems only marginally related to the curriculum--problems of racial difficulty, problems of class-adjustment. In discussing the educational priorities of city schools, it was generally agreed among the speakers that these matters would be thought of here as subordinate. That is, they would take the rather old-fashioned view that the school is still an institution dedicated to the training of the mind and that the priorities are still educational.

Fantini, Mario D. THE REFORM OF URBAN SCHOOLS, SCHOOLS FOR THE 70'S. Washington, D.C.: National Education Association, 1970. (ED 047 042)

In this book, an overall analysis of the urban crisis is presented and concrete suggestions are made for renewing urban education through a unique design called the "public-schools-of-choice system." Fundamentally a plan in which a range of optional school programs would be offered to diverse student groups in every community, the public schools of choice would open up a range of educational opportunity and choice so far available mainly to students attending private schools.

Fantini, Mario D., and Weinstein, Gerald. THE DISADVANTAGED: CHALLENGE TO EDUCATION. New York: Harper and Row, 1968.

The authors include as disadvantaged any child for whom the established educational process and curriculum is outdated or irrelevant. They seem to place blame on our system of education in all schools, not just the inner city. This is a comprehensive work which states the problem and goes on to suggest changes and strategies for presenting these changes. Recommended is a relevant, diversified curriculum based on three arenas: academic content, individual talents, and group interaction.

Farber, Bernard. "Compensatory Education and Social Justice." THE EDUCATION DIGEST 100 (March 1972): 17–22.

This article discusses the inability of many compensatory programs to help the culturally-deprived youth. It also discusses how society has created the culturally disadvantaged student, which effectively prevents any real growth from taking place.

Firman, William D., et al. MULTISTATE CONFERENCE TO STRENGTHEN STATE-LOCAL RELATIONSHIPS IN URBAN EDUCATION (NEW YORK CITY, 27–30 NOVEMBER 1966). Pts. 1 and 2. Albany: New York State Education Department, 1967. (ED 017 969)

Part 1 of the document summarizes the topics which are presented verbatim in part 2. Topics discussed include: (1) urban education and the demonstration cities program, (2) research and development groups, and the state and urban situations, (3) inadequacies of present city and state programs for the financial support of education in urban areas, (4) legal structure of state education departments in relation to assisting urban areas, (5) the increasing interrelationship of state education departments and other agencies of state and federal government, and (6) education in the large cities in the future.

Fleischer, Susan. "Lots of Paperback Books: A Help for Reading Problems in Poverty Area Schools." JOURNAL OF LEARNING DISABILITIES 5 (June 1972): 367–69.

Schools, particularly in poverty areas, should fill their classrooms and libraries with paperback editions possessing high interest and low reading levels. This available reading can improve students' reading motivation, competence, and independence. This bank of data is, therefore, put at the disposal of the teaching profession to encourage factor analysis studies in depth by research students at the masters and doctoral levels.

Forbes, Roy H. "The Louisville Urban Education Center." JOURNAL OF RE-
SEARCH AND DEVELOPMENT 5 (Summer 1972): 98-103.

> This article reviews the establishment of the Louisville Urban Edu-
> cation Center. The center is separate from the three sponsoring
> institutions, the Louisville Public School System, the University of
> Louisville, and the University of Kentucky. The purpose of the
> center is to facilitate services delivered between the universities
> and the school system, to provide support for research and develop-
> ment, to offer services for strategic planning, and to provide an
> information base for facilitation of all services. The difficulty of
> organizing the center, as well as the plan for future operations, is
> candidly discussed.

Frost, Joe L., and Hawkes, Glenn R. THE DISADVANTAGED CHILD: ISSUES
AND INNOVATIONS. Boston: Houghton Mifflin Co., 1966.

> This book of readings is offered to provide a needed reference for
> a wide segment of the population. It should help teachers, stu-
> dents, and other interested citizens to understand what is involved
> in the creation of a desirable environment for disadvantaged chil-
> dren, and to discover ways in which they can help to foster healthy
> and beneficial programs for these young people.

Furno, Orlando F. CULTURALLY DISADVANTAGED CHILDREN: PUPIL DATA
BANK. Baltimore, Md.: Early School Admissions Project, Baltimore Public
Schools, 1967.

> This bank of data is put at the disposal of the teaching profession
> to encourage factor analysis studies in-depth by research students
> at the masters and doctoral levels.

Getzels, J.W. "Education for the Inner City: A Practical Proposal by an Im-
practical Theorist." Address given at the American Association of School Administrators, Atlantic City, New Jersey, 13 February 1967. (ED 025 451)

> The position of this address is that urban education problems require
> long-term conceptual analysis leading to reconstruction. Focused
> preparation is necessary, that is, prospective teachers, counselors,
> psychologists, and administrators must learn to understand each
> other's problems and functions. They also need to understand the
> educational and other issues confronting each other in the inner
> city, so they can cooperate more effectively in the school situa-
> tion.

Glassman, Alan M., and Belasco, James A. "Appealed Grievances in Urban
Education." EDUCATION AND URBAN SOCIETY 7 (November 1974): 73-87.

> An examination of the nature and use of appealed grievances in an
> urban school district indicated that the grievance appeals process
> was being utilized by the leaders of the teacher organization to

enhance their organization's status. Classroom conditions were found to be a likely area of future conflict and implications are discussed for the training of local representatives for more effective participation in the bargaining process.

Gunderson, Keith. MENTALITY AND MACHINES. Garden City, N.Y.: Anchor Books, 1971.

Computer science in the twentieth century has forced philosophers to redraw the line between man and machines in a variety of respects giving a "suburban status" to the hallowed credos of mechanistic materialism. The most important implication that computer science has had for philosophy is the new insights it provides for old concepts.

Hall, Shirley M. LABORATORY FOR CHANGE--THE MADISON AREA PROJECT. SUMMER REPORT. Syracuse, N.Y.: Syracuse City School District, 1964. (ED 001 655)

The project had its beginning at one junior high school. Attention was focused on the variety of urban problems which cause educational disadvantagement. Teacher preparation, desegregation, preschool training, curriculum development, student motivation, and school dropouts were identified as some of the major areas in need of greater attention.

Hardy, William G., ed. COMMUNICATION AND THE DISADVANTAGED CHILD. Baltimore, Md.: Williams and Wilkins, Co., 1970.

This is a collection of different points of view by well-known authorities on the teaching of the disadvantaged. It is hoped that some clear, fundamental concepts are conveyed for future service.

Havighurst, Robert J.. DEVELOPMENTAL TASKS AND EDUCATION. 2d ed. New York: David McKay Co., 1952.

This is a brief, 100-page booklet tracing human development from infancy through adulthood. Several chapters include material pertinent to those working with middle-school disadvantaged children.

_____. "The Politics of Big City Education." Paper presented at the annual convention of the American Association of School Administrators, Atlantic City, New Jersey, 20 February 1976. (ED 117 855)

Politics is used in a broad sense to refer to the social, economic, political, and civil forces that impinge on the publicly-financed school system. These forces are generated both from outside and inside the educational system. It is the author's view that the big cities and the school systems of most of these cities are in enough trouble that will force action by the people and that much of the trouble will be solved in the next twenty-five years through joint citizen-educator efforts.

Hemsing, Esther D., ed. JOB CORPS: AN EDUCATIONAL ALTERNATIVE. Washington, D.C.: American Association of Colleges for Teacher Education, 1971. (ED 080 488)

The Job Corps Student Teaching Project is a combined effort of Job Corps and the American Association of Colleges for Teacher Education. This document describes methods of recruitment and selection orientation, supervision, project seminars, etc.

Himes, Joseph S. "Negro Teen-Age Culture." ISSUES IN ADOLESCENT PSY-CHOLOGY. New York: Meredith Corp., 1969.

The author feels that the aggression shown by black youth has two modes: personal aggression among lower-class youth and the racial protest movement among college youth. He feels that the street as a social institution is an important factor in their culture.

Hirsch, Werner Z. PLANNING EDUCATION TODAY AND TOMORROW. Los Angeles: California University, Institute of Government and Public Affairs, 1966. (ED 019 757)

In three areas of responsibility--policy consideration, program formulation, and program administration--educational planners are relatively unprepared to make decisions affecting urban education in both the immediate and the distant future.

Hummel, Raymond C., and Nagle, John M. URBAN EDUCATION IN AMERICA: PROBLEMS AND PROSPECTS. Fair Lawn, N.Y.: Oxford University Press, 1973. (ED 079 439)

This book tries to provide a systematic and comprehensive view of the condition of urban education in the 1970s.

Hunt, J. McVicker. HUMAN INTELLIGENCE. New Brunswick, N.J.: Transaction Books, 1972.

Originally published in TRANSACTION MAGAZINE, this work concerns real world problems and searches out practical solutions. It concerns the social changes and policies that have aroused long-standing and present-day needs and anxieties.

Janowitz, Morris. INSTITUTION BUILDING IN URBAN EDUCATION. New York: Russell Sage Foundation, 1969. (ED 041 959)

For annotation see section D, Janowitz, Morris.

Jayatilleke, Raja, comp. ALTERNATIVE SCHOOLING. New York: Columbia University, ERIC Clearinghouse on the Urban Disadvantaged, 1976. (ED 128 495)

    This is the second of a series of capsule bibliographies on current issues on urban and minority education.

_____. COLLEGIATE COMPENSATORY PROGRAMS. New York: Columbia University, ERIC Clearinghouse on the Urban Disadvantaged, 1976. (ED 128 498)

    This is the fifth in a series of capsule bibliographies on current issues in urban and minority education.

_____. GROUPING PRACTICES. New York: Columbia University, ERIC Clearinghouse on the Urban Disadvantaged, 1976. (ED 128 494)

    This is the first of a series of capsule bibliographies on current issues in urban and minority education.

_____. HUMAN RELATIONS IN THE CLASSROOM. New York: Columbia University, ERIC Clearinghouse on the Urban Disadvantaged, 1976. (ED 128 496)

    This is the third of a series of capsule bibliographies on current issues in urban and minority education.

_____. THE LAW, THE COURTS, AND MINORITY GROUP EDUCATION. New York: Columbia University, ERIC Clearinghouse on the Urban Disadvantaged, 1976. (ED 128 497)

    This is the fourth of a series of capsule bibliographies on current issues in urban and minority education.

Jessen, David L. EDUCATION IN THE BIG CITIES: PROBLEMS AND PROSPECTS. REPORT NO. 63. Denver: Education Commission of the States, 1975. (ED 118 696)

    Some of the current thinking on planning and effecting improvements in education in the big cities is brought together under four major chapters in this publication.

Johnson, John L. "Special Education and the Inner City: A Challenge for the Future or Another Means for Cooling the Mark Out?" JOURNAL OF SPECIAL EDUCATION 3 (Fall 1969): 241-51.

Joseph, Stephen M., ed. THE ME NOBODY KNOWS. New York: Avon Books, 1969.

    Edited by a teacher, this anthology of children's writing illustrates that teachers can learn much about their students by providing them with similar writing experiences and that approaches to reaching disadvantaged children vary, requiring teacher ingenuity rather than reliance on stereotype. Though developed from the city ghetto, its message is safely generalizable to other areas where the disadvantaged reside.

Kozol, Jonathan. "Halls of Darkness: In the Ghetto Schools." HARVARD EDUCATIONAL REVIEW 37 (Summer 1967): 379-407.

This excerpt from Kozol's book, "Death at an Early Age," places the blame for apathy and lack of educational progress which blacks exhibit in the schools on teachers who give lip service to equality but who, in fact, are very prejudiced. The message is powerful and is overwhelmingly critical of the teaching profession.

Lauwerys, Joseph, and Scanlon, David G., eds. EDUCATION IN CITIES: THE WORLD YEAR BOOK OF EDUCATION, 1970. New York: Harcourt, Brace and World, 1970.

The purpose of this book is to concentrate on the effects of urbanization on education at all levels--an aspect which has, of course, been mentioned explicitly in the literature concerned with problems of urban growth, though usually in the context of social problems, town planning, etc. What is attempted in this volume, therefore, is to present a comparative study of some general educational problems common to most urban areas and then to see what particular problems arise from different sorts of urban development.

Lazerson, Marvin. ORIGINS OF URBAN EDUCATION-PUBLIC EDUCATION IN MASSACHUSETTS, 1870-1915. Cambridge, Mass.: Harvard University Press, 1971.

The author asserts that between the years 1870-1915 the public school system was established. The basic assumption of the time was that the poor fail their children. Therefore the decisions on education were made by expert educators. The cycle of reform is based on the fact that assumptions were made upon which decisions were made. When the results were ineffectual, the whole process was regenerated. The cycle is noted to have initial goals degenerate and then transformed into different goals that may have become permanently implanted in the institution.

Lea, Jeanne E. "Mirror, Mirror on the Wall." ENGLISH JOURNAL 61 (November 1972): 1239-43.

Lea discusses problems of present and future urban educators specifically in the inner city, and makes specific reference to the fact that the problems involve ethnic and racial differences.

Levine, Daniel U. "Moving Toward a Dead End in Big Cities?" INTEGRATED EDUCATION 7 (March-April 1969): 40-45.

The author reviews trends in Kansas City, Missouri, considering the social and political forces which affect integration policy in major metropolitan areas. The need for change in the school system is focused upon the classroom teacher in the inner city. This approach and the resulting difficulties are reflected upon by the author.

_____. "The Reform of Urban Education." PHI DELTA KAPPAN 52 (February 1971): 328-33.

The examination of problems in urban education is presented with the historical referents of this system. Institutional overload and its effects on urban schools whose resources are limited is a key component in the deliberation. The organizational response to achieving educational goals is carefully analyzed. The conceptual analysis and practical examples of solution provide educators with useful information on institutional rebuilding. Urban education problems require comprehensive recognition of the totality of the enterprise. This holistic approach is adequately made.

Levy, Jerald E. GHETTO SCHOOL: CLASS WARFARE IN AN ELEMENTARY SCHOOL. New York: Pegasus, Western Publishing Co., 1970. (ED 050 199)

This is a participant-observer's description and analysis of an American ghetto school. In the context of sociopolitical realities, the impact of the school is considered. The social implications, the role of teachers, and the racial dimension of teaching are included in the discussion.

Lindsay, J.V. "Urban Education-Where We Are Going." INTELLECT 101 (1972): 84-87.

A LONG RANGE PLAN FOR IMPROVING EDUCATION AND URBAN LIFE IN ST. PAUL, MINNESOTA. St. Paul, Minn.: Saint Paul Public Schools, 1969. (ED 037 086)

The study contains 200 recommendations for overhauling the educational facilities in St. Paul, Minnesota, and also envisions an overhauling of the structure of the community itself.

McCoy, Rhody Arnold, Jr. "Analysis of Critical Issues and Incidents in the New York City School Crisis, 1967-1970, and Their Implications for Urban Education in the 1970's." Ed.D. dissertation, University of Massachusetts, 1971.

Ocean Hill Brownsville Demonstration School is the subject material of this dissertation. This study used panel discussions of many of the persons involved to analyze the attempts at educational improvement. The author analyzes the data and concludes that educational reform, in order to occur, requires a violent revolution.

McKelvey, Troy V., and Swanson, Austin D. THE UNIQUE PROBLEMS OF
URBAN SCHOOL ADMINISTRATION: AN INSTITUTE FOR SCHOOL ADMIN-
ISTRATORS OF THE BUFFALO PUBLIC SCHOOLS AND SEVERAL SUBURBAN
SCHOOL DISTRICTS. Buffalo: State University of New York-Buffalo, Depart-
ment of Educational Administration, 1967. (ED 045 739)

> This report on an institute for school administrators in Buffalo, New
> York, focuses on the problems of urban school administration. The
> State University of New York-Buffalo, the Buffalo Public Schools,
> and several suburban schools came together in order to enhance the
> quality and creative potential of educators, and to exchange ideas
> on the problems of urban schools.

Mar, Barry Malcolm. "Urban Education: A Syndetic Inquiry." Ph.D. dissertation, University of Wisconsin-Milwaukee, 1974.

> The purpose of this study is a review of the state of the art of ur-
> ban education and its prospects for the future. An attempt at def-
> inition, goals, and objectives as well as needs for the develop-
> ment of the field are investigated. The author surveyed and ana-
> lyzed literature and concluded that the characteristics of urban
> education are: (1) lack of definitions for the field, (2) problems
> and processes are interrelated with other disciplines, and (3)
> greater professional attention to the development of multidisciplinary
> approaches to urban education has and is occurring.

Marcus, Sheldon, and Vairo, Phillip D., comp. URBAN EDUCATION: CRISIS
OR OPPORTUNITY. Metuchen, N.J.: Scarecrow Press, 1972.

> This book contains the current views of educators on community
> control, segregation, alternative schools, urban education, and
> other timely issues. An extensive bibliography is provided.

Mohl, Raymond A. "Alice Barrows and the Platoon School Plan." URBAN EDU-
CATION IN THE TWENTIETH CENTURY (October 1974): 213-37.

> This article discusses the platoon schools of Gary, Indiana in the
> period from 1906 to 1938. This platoon school combined a wide
> range of reforms advocated by progressives of the time. Alice
> Barrows attempted to initiate this idea into the New York City
> school system. The platoon plan and the contributions of Alice
> Barrows are reviewed.

NEW RELATIONSHIPS IN INSTRUCTIONAL TELEVISION, PROCEEDINGS OF
THE CONFERENCE JOINTLY SPONSORED BY THE EDUCATION SECTION OF
THE ELECTRONIC INDUSTRIES ASSOCIATION AND THE INSTRUCTIONAL DI-
VISION OF THE NATIONAL ASSOCIATION OF EDUCATIONAL BROADCAS-
TERS. Washington, D.C.: Educational Media Council, April 1967.

> This is a collection of speeches that examine current issues and
> trends in education as they relate to ITV. Topics discussed include

the status of ITV, curriculum and organizational patterns, history, accomplishments, and the utilization of the services of the Metropolitan Area Council for ITV Resources.

O'Brien, Richard J. COST MODEL FOR LARGE URBAN SCHOOLS. Washington, D.C.: National Center for Educational Statistics, 1967. (ED 013 527)

This document contains a cost submodel of an urban educational system. This model requires that the pupil population and proposed school building are known.

Ornstein, Allan C., et al., eds. EDUCATING THE DISADVANTAGED: SCHOOL YEAR 1969-1970. Vol. 2, parts 1 and 2. New York: AMS Press, 1971. (ED 050 224)

This is a collection of essays which are from magazine and journal articles published in 1969-70. The purpose is to assist educators in keeping up with recent literature. Part 1 is concerned with "Who are the Disadvantaged." Part 2 is concerned with "Class, Race, and Psychology."

Parsons, John M. AN ASSESSMENT OF STATE FUNDING AND METROPOLITAN OVERBURDEN RELATED TO URBAN, URBAN-RURAL, AND RURAL SCHOOL DISTRICTS IN FLORIDA. Miami: Dade County Public Schools, 1971. (ED 058 662)

This report documents the municipal overburden, the lack of state support in urban counties when compared to rural counties, and the educational needs of urban areas.

PARTNERS FOR EDUCATIONAL REFORM AND RENEWAL. Toledo, Ohio: Toledo University, College of Education, 1973. (ED 087 716)

The strategy of the Ohio model is to produce able teachers through the utilization of competency-based preservice teacher education programs, while also implementing inservice programs that introduce and support educational innovation, such as individually-guided education and multiunit schools. The teacher education center is the conceptual and physical link in the model, tying together the university and the school systems.

Passow, A. Harry, ed. URBAN EDUCATION IN THE 1970'S: REFLECTIONS AND A LOOK AHEAD. New York: Teachers College Press, 1971. (ED 054 290)

This is a compilation of a series of lectures given to provide perspective on developments in urban education that can serve as a basis for projecting the direction in the 1970s.

Passow, A. Harry, and Goldberg, Miriam. EDUCATION OF THE DISADVANTAGED. New York: Holt, Rinehart and Winston, 1967.

A book of readings which represents current thinking and, wherever possible, research concerning the educational problems of disadvantaged pupils. The papers deal with both the theoretical issues such as possible social and psychological causes as well as antecedents of observed learning deficits and practical school problems, such as the use of intelligence tests for predicting academic achievement and the design of special programs to deal with widespread educational retardation in depressed areas.

Porter, John W. "Jobs, Dollars and Race From an Educator's Perspective: Urban Education in a Pluralistic Society." Speech delivered before the annual meeting of the National Urban League, Atlanta, Georgia, July 1975. (ED 124 670)

The main message of this paper is that 1975 ushered in a new and different way of thinking and reacting to public education at all levels as well as reflecting attitudes of consumerism, confrontation, and conciliation.

PREDICTING PUPIL YIELD BY TYPES OF DWELLING UNITS. Towson, Md.: Baltimore County Board of Education, 1961. (ED 035 162)

This publication presents procedures for estimating future pupil yield from new housing developments. This should make possible good administrative decisions as to the location and design of school buildings.

Raynor, John, and Harden, Jane, eds. CITIES, COMMUNITIES AND THE YOUNG. Vol. 1. Milton Keynes, Engl.: Open University Press, 1973.

This is a selection of twenty-eight articles which provide insight on the important issues confronting urban society. Articles are from leading writers in the area of urban education: James S. Coleman, Frank Reissman, Martin Deutsch, Mario D. Fantini, and Gerald Weinstein.

Redfern, George B. "Monitoring the Urban Education Front." Paper presented at the 101st annual meeting of the American Association of School Administrators, Atlantic City, New Jersey, February 1969. (ED 027 636)

Big-city administrators face a multitude of problems falling under three general headings--finance, discontent, and educational programs.

Reller, Theodore L. EDUCATIONAL ADMINISTRATION IN METROPOLITAN AREAS. Bloomington, Ind.: Phi Delta Kappa, 1974. (ED 102 664)

The position of this publication is that metropolitan areas may provide an administrative structure for renewing educational administrative alternatives.

Riessman, Frank. THE CULTURALLY DEPRIVED CHILD. New York: Harper and Row, 1962.

This is considered one of the foremost works in the field. Riessman's discussion and suggestions are capable of generalization to
rural as well as urban areas.

Riles, Wilson C. THE URBAN EDUCATION TASK FORCE REPORT. FINAL
REPORT ON THE TASK FORCE ON URBAN EDUCATION TO THE DEPART-
MENT OF HEALTH, EDUCATION AND WELFARE. New York: Praeger, 1970.

The Riles Report brings forth a set of proposals to make public school
systems, through national goals and policy, an instrument for "up
and out of poverty in a generation." He proposes the Urban Education Act which would tie funds to performance criteria. The
Riles Report focuses on the financial need of fiscally disadvantaged
urban schools. The report proposes alternatives to public school
systems. He outlines the failures of education in terms of absence
of clearly stated policy and methods for implementing policy. The
proposals are impressive, although disclaimed by educators.

Rippey, Robert M. REPORT OF AN URBAN EDUCATION REFORM EXPERI-
MENT: PROBLEMS AND PROMISES. SECTION II: PROJECT EVALUATION.
Chicago: University of Illinois at Chicago Circle Campus, 1972. (ED 087 746)

This report tells of the efforts of an urban college of education
to develop a cooperative program in urban teacher education.
Given is the origin of the project, operational problems, solutions
attempted, and critical functions of systematic evaluation. Statements of conclusion by the development coordinator are also included.

Rosen, Bernard C. "Race, Ethnicity, and the Achievement Syndrome." AMERI-
CAN SOCIOLOGICAL REVIEW 24 (1959): 47-60 .

The psychological and cultural orientation of six ethnic-racial
groups is measured in relation to achievement.

Shaw, Fredrick. "The Educational Park in New York, Archetype of the School
of the Future?" PHI DELTA KAPPAN 50 (February 1969): 329-31.

Shrag, Peter, and Roberts, Wallace. "You Don't Have to Leave School to
Drop Out." SATURDAY REVIEW, 21 March 1970, pp. 59-61, 78.

This article describes some of today's schools as irrelevant to the
student's life-style and needs, and as a result many students are
dropouts two years before they actually drop out.

Sloane, Martin E. "Milliken V. Bradley in Perspective." JOURNAL OF LAW
AND EDUCATION 4 (January 1975): 209-13.

Sloane suggests that the Milliken decision focused the court's attention on the interrelationship between school segregation and residential

segregation, and may have laid the basis for successful legal action in the future.

"Symposium Participants React: Urban Education: Revolution and Renewal. Symposium Discussion." NATIONAL ELEMENTARY PRINCIPAL 51 (April 1972): 19-57.

Thomas, Thomas C. ON IMPROVING URBAN SCHOOL FACILITIES AND EDUCATION. Menlo Park, Calif.: Stanford Research Institution Educational Policy Research Center, 1969. (ED 041 094)

> Explorations of a broad range of alternative policies for urban school facilities and education are presented rather than attempting to design the "best" policy. Broad perspectives on school construction decisions relative to analyzation of goals, stakeholders' positions, and implementation of actions are presented. Questions of financing, construction and school location in relationship to environmental factors are considered. The study concludes that innovations considered offer promise to education.

Tucker, Sterling. WHY THE GHETTO MUST GO. New York: National Board, Young Men's Christian Association, 1968.

> The pamphlet is abstracted from Sterling Tucker's book, "Beyond the Burning: Life and Death of the Ghetto." Its message is that hope for the black person must be achieved through actual integration in living situations, employment opportunities, and educational facilities. The author gives a strong justification for the behavior of the black person who has been conditioned to life through slum living.

URBAN SCHOOL CRISIS: THE PROBLEM AND SOLUTIONS PROPOSED BY THE HEW URBAN EDUCATION TASK FORCE. Washington, D.C.: National School Public Relations Association, 1970. (ED 041 080)

> This report, compiled by the Urban Education Task Force (under the Department of Health, Education, and Welfare), offers both a comprehensive analysis of the crisis in urban education and recommendations for the future.

Walberg, Herbert J., and Kopan, Andrew T. RETHINKING URBAN EDUCATION. San Francisco: Jossey-Bass, 1972.

> This book provides a collection of empirical evidence, evaluation, and input from a variety of disciplines for use by planners and administrators. This work provides a focus as its title indicates. The treatment of urban education as a generic term weakens some of the ability of the application of materials presented. However, such a collection of studies and works devoted to the problem of urban education is valuable as a resource for administrators.

Wayson, William W. "Guidelines for Resolving Some Urgent Problems in Urban Education." URBAN EDUCATION 7 (July 1972): 109-17.

The basic problems in urban education are poverty, inadequate and crowded housing, unequal opportunity, white prejudice, black prejudice, urban flight, professional inability to resolve problems, city finance, suburban strangulation, and statewide antiurban politics. The author calls for systematic and comprehensive planning and implementation of methods to offset these first order problems.

Williams, Thomas R. "Dimensions of Autonomy in Urban Education: Current Trends and Some Radical Implications." INTERCHANGE 4 (1973): 77-88.

Major current uses of the term "autonomy" are reviewed to make explicit the major referent bases implicit in the literature. The implications of changes in these bases for future change in education are discussed.

Woock, Roger R., ed. EDUCATION AND THE URBAN CRISIS. Scranton, Pa.: International Textbook Co., 1970. (ED 050 223)

This is a collection of essays on problems of education in relation to the urban crisis. The analysis of school decentralization in New York City, urban community problems, disadvantaged youth, teachers in urban schools, and school organization are treated.

Part II
URBAN HIGHER EDUCATION

America's grand experiment in mass higher education through the G.I. Bill following World War II, which coincided with the technological explosion of the
1950s, laid the foundations for what has been called the third era in higher
education. The first era was devoted to preparation of the social elite, and
the second, relying on the land grant universities, provided for the selective
education of potential leaders from and for a growing middle class, industrial
nation.

The third era opened higher education to all classes and is characterized by
the concept of continuing and recurrent education for both youth and adults
throughout life. It is advanced education for a society that demands more and
more credentials, that demands a continuing updating of skills, and is impatient
with time-honored assumptions and traditions of the academy. Application of
knowledge is increasingly recognized as the criterion of its worth, not knowledge
for knowledge's sake. A better-educated adult population with more leisure,
faced with the obsolete knowledge, is willing and able to devote its time and
resources to education on a part-time basis. It has, however, its own views
about not only how education should be used but also how it should be conducted. It is a citizenry that understands that higher education institutions
exist not by divine right but at the discretion of the society.

Part 2 begins with higher education's most drastic break with its past in accept-
ing and promoting nontraditional or external degrees and programs for a student
population it had never solicited before. The assault on the urban university's
ivory tower from its host community, the expectations for the university to per-
form a responsible citizenship role, a demand that it acknowledge the right of
access and success for urban minorities, are among the issues identified here.
Finally, for those who have responsibility for institutional personnel performance,
this part offers references related to efforts by higher education to prepare its
own staffs and personnel in other institutions, organizations, and agencies.

Section A

NONTRADITIONAL PROGRAMS AND DEGREES

Burt, Samuel M., and Striner, Herbert E. THE EXTERNAL DEGREE AND HIGHER EDUCATION IN THE UNITED STATES: AN IN-DEPTH OVERVIEW AS THE BASIS FOR A NON-RADICAL INDEPENDENT STUDIES PROGRAM FOR AN URBAN UNIVERSITY. Washington, D.C.: American University, College of Continuing Education, 1972. (ED 067 989)

> This report discusses the various interpretations of the external de-
> gree concept, its potential impact on American higher education,
> and how an urban university may expand and improve its delivery
> systems to a larger variety of student populations on a sound finan-
> cial basis.

Dawson, Helaine. ON THE OUTSKIRTS OF HOPE: EDUCATING YOUTH FROM POVERTY AREAS. New York: McGraw-Hill Book Co., 1968.

> This book takes the reader into a classroom to observe real situa-
> tions and real people. The author's reflections and discussions are
> based on firsthand experience with 200 young people over a three-
> year period.

Dentler, Robert A. BIG CITY DROPOUTS AND ILLITERATES. New York: New York Center for Urban Education, 1968.

> The problems of urban area dropouts and illiterates are thoroughly
> researched and documented in this book. In statistical form, com-
> parisons of dropouts, employment, and other facets of the dropout
> problem are explored.

Eriksen, Aase. SCATTERED SCHOOLS. Philadelphia: University of Pennsylvania, 1971. (ED 061 880)

> This document describes a model (the PASS Model) that allows for
> universities to develop programs and facilities that are of mutual
> benefit to the university and to the community of which it is a
> part.

Fisher, Francis D. AN IMPRESSION OF 'THE OAKLAND PROJECT'--CONSID-
ERATIONS IMPORTANT TO THE DESIGN OF PROJECTS LINKING UNIVERSI-
TIES AND CITY GOVERNMENT. Washington, D.C.: Urban Institute, 1972.

> For five years graduate students in the Oakland Project of the Uni-
> versity of California at Berkeley had been working at jobs in the
> city of Oakland while continuing their studies. The paper describes
> the Oakland Project and seeks to extract from it considerations im-
> portant to the design of any university-city relationship. In this
> project students were candidates for Ph.D. degrees in political sci-
> ence. Their city jobs provided useful vantage points for student
> study as well as rendering modest assistance to the city.

Gold, Lawrence N. COLLEGE STUDENTS IN LOCAL GOVERNMENT: THE
URBAN CORPS APPROACH. Washington, D.C.: International City Management
Association, 1972. (ED 071 544)

> Public service internships not only provide a means for college stu-
> dents to help government get its job done, they also teach the stu-
> dent a good deal about the real world of urban affairs. This re-
> port covers the Urban Corps approach to providing a college student
> internship program in local government.

Gordon, Edmund W. VOCATIONAL-TECHNICAL EDUCATION FOR THE DIS-
ADVANTAGED. Columbus, Ohio: Center for Vocational and Technical Education, 1968.

> This is preliminary material related to the National Vocational-
> Technical Teacher Education Seminar of October 1968 in Chicago.
> The author writes that it should be the goals of vocational educa-
> tion to develop in the student the ability, understanding, attitudes,
> work habits, and appreciation which are needed by a human being
> to live a meaningful life and to make a productive contribution to
> the society in which he lives.

A GUIDE TO THE DEVELOPMENT OF VOCATIONAL EDUCATION PROGRAMS
AND SERVICES FOR THE DISADVANTAGED. Washington, D.C.: National
Committee on Employment of Youth, October 1969.

> This is an explanation of the 1968 Vocational Education Amend-
> ment and how it related to the disadvantaged. Who are the dis-
> advantaged? The disadvantaged student will progress in direct
> ratio to the kind and quality of instruction he receives. Use of
> instructional techniques and materials should be simple and realis-
> tic when planning curriculum for this student.

House, Peter. DEVELOPMENT OF METROPOLITAN (CITY III) MODEL. FINAL
REPORT. Washington, D.C.: Envirometrics, 1970. (ED 048 774)

> CITY III, a computer-assisted simulation model to be used in the

study of complex interactions and consequences of public and private decision making in an urban setting, is described in this report.

Johnson, Byron. THE VITALITY OF A CITY: CHALLENGE TO HIGHER EDUCATION; CHALLENGE TO EDUCATION: A NEW APPROACH. San Francisco: California University, Medical Center, 1967. (ED 024 346)

The author identifies how the urban American university must change from its European model.

Keefer, Daryle E. "A Study of Evening Institutions of Higher Education in the Large Metropolitan Communities." Ph.D. dissertation, Northwestern University, 1946.

Covering six major metropolitan areas, Keefer surveyed thirty-six institutions of higher learning which had evening programs offering college credit.

Kerr, Clark. "The Urban-Grant University: A Model for the Future." Lecture given to the centennial meeting of the City College Chapter of Phi Beta Kappa, New York, 18 October 1935. (ED 025 198)

The author states that many U.S. colleges and universities, including some in urban settings, are apparently less concerned with urban problems today than they were a third of a century ago. There is a growing need for a new kind of university that would aggressively approach city problems, such as an urban-grant university. This institution would become directly involved in improving the total urban environment—architecture, use of space, health, poverty, cultural and educational equality, and recreational programs—and thus bridge the gap between campus and community.

Lavell, Martha, and Rosenbaum, Patricia. "Studying Urban Problems by Mail." ADULT LEADERSHIP 20 (October 1971): 142.

This is a description of a program developed by the University of Pennsylvania entitled Suburban Potential Program. The project was developed for women who were concerned about urban problems, race relations, and the increasing black-white polarization in the United States.

Leinwand, Gerald. "Needed: A College of Public Education and Service." SOCIOLOGY OF EDUCATION 34 (March 1970): 305-10.

This is a concrete description of the components and operation of an institution responsive to community needs and based on a new pattern of teacher education, one which the author envisions as the logical next step in urban higher education.

Lieberman, Janet E. "The Middle College High School: A New Model for Re-mediation." Paper presented at the annual meeting of the International Reading Association, New York City, 13 May 1975. (ED 105 419)

> To motivate the urban adolescent, to offer a program of skills geared to work and life, and to reduce the need for remediation at the college level, LaGuardia (New York) Community College estab-lished a middle college, a new educational subunit, to cover the last three years of secondary school as well as the community col-lege sequence with a program that focuses on remediation and career education.

Lipsky, Michael, ed. SYNOPSIS OF UPWARD BOUND WINTER CONFERENCE. Conference held in New Orleans, Louisiana, 16-18 January 1968. Washington, D.C.: Office of Economic Opportunity, 1968. (ED 021 931)

> This document is an edited transcript of speeches and other pro-ceedings from the 1968 New Orleans Upward Bound Conference dealing with the response to the urban crisis and issues related to black power.

Liveright, A. A. THE UNCOMMON COLLEGE, THE COLLEGE OF CONTINU-ING EDUCATION AT METROPOLIS UNIVERSITY. Boston: Center for the Study of Liberal Education for Adults at Boston University, 1966. (ED 018 697)

> Here is described hypothetical Metropolis University of 1980 with an undergraduate curriculum designed to provide a climate for life-long learning and with a College of Continuing Education devel-oped along lines of the four primary roles of adults--worker, family member, citizen, and self-realizing individual.

Marshak, Robert E. "Problems and Prospects of an Urban Public University." DAEDALUS 104 (Winter 1975): 192-201.

> The author discusses the need for a complete reassessment of educa-tional priorities for the urban university. Three goals are empha-sized: inclusion of academically-unprepared individuals in the uni-versity, development of academic curricula relevant to urban prob-lems, and development of research and service in areas related to the needs of the urban community.

Murphy, Thomas P. "Free Universities and Urban Higher Education." In his UNIVERSITIES IN URBAN CRISIS, pp. 113-35. New York: Dunellen Publish-ing, 1975.

> Because students in the 1960s felt that their curricula was not rele-vant and slow to change, the free university movement began. The types, goals, operation, and curricula are discussed. An evalua-tion and prognosis of the free university movement follow.

Neidhart, Anthony C., ed. CONTINUING EDUCATION FOR TEXAS: SPE-
CIAL STUDIES OF NON-TRADITIONAL APPROACHES TO EDUCATION. Austin,
Tex.: University of Texas, 1974. (ED 105 193)

> The report presents thirteen studies, undertaken by Texas institutions
> of higher learning, to consider needs for improved delivery systems
> of higher education services to adults and adult continuing educa-
> tion programs.

Park, Young. A CONCEPTUAL BASIS FOR NON-TRADITIONAL STUDY AND
ALTERNATIVES IN THE ESTABLISHMENT OF A NON-TRADITIONAL STUDY.
Berkeley, Calif.: Peralta College, 1975. (ED 104 467)

> Traditional educational methods can no longer effectively meet the
> various needs and demands of the many diverse groups and individ-
> uals found in large metropolitan multicampus districts. Existing ur-
> ban community colleges do not provide alternative services because
> they are limited in flexibility by state statutes and by the traditions
> of academia. Thus, a nontraditional college must be established as
> a separate entity to supplement and complement the offerings of ex-
> isting institutions.

Perry, Charles E. "The First Thousand Days." Speech presented before the
Florida State Board of Regents, 6 July 1972.

> This document presents a speech by the president of Florida Inter-
> national University concerning the creation of the institution. Flor-
> ida International is an upper-level college located outside of Miami.
> The institution has been innovative in its physical structure as well
> as in its educational philosophy. Located at the side of the aban-
> doned Tamiami Airport, the institution has utilized the control tower
> and old hangars as administrative and faculty office buildings.

ROGER WILLIAMS COLLEGE UNIVERSITY WITHOUT WALLS URBAN STUDIES
CENTER. Bristol, R.I.: Roger Williams College, 1972. (ED 074 899)

> Roger Williams College is one of twenty colleges and universities
> engaged in a new cooperative educational venture that offers an
> alternative approach to obtaining a college degree. The program,
> called the University Without Walls, is designed to provide mature
> students with new learning opportunities in higher education outside
> of the traditional educational mainstream.

Spear, George E. "The University and Adult Education." In UNIVERSITIES
IN THE URBAN CRISIS, edited by Thomas P. Murphy, pp. 181-96. New York:
Dunellen Publishing, 1975.

> For this discussion, adult higher education is referred to as continu-
> ing education and/or extension, and universities are defined as ur-
> ban if they are located in urban areas. Extension or continuing
> education divisions have espoused the philosophy and practice of

nontraditional education. The major problem in creating nontraditional, community orientation for the university is the institutional organization.

_____. "The University Public Service Mission." In UNIVERSITIES IN THE URBAN CRISIS, edited by Thomas P. Murphy, pp. 95-111. New York: Dunellen Publishing, 1975.

The university became actively involved with the urban community because of legislation passed in 1965. The two basic types of programs were those which were community-oriented and those which focused on the individual. In this chapter programs are described and evaluated. Also, recommendations for the future are made.

Spector, N. J. "Continuing Education and Training for Urban Administrators: A Look at a New Interdisciplinary Approach." ADULT LEADERSHIP 23 (December 1974): 170-74.

The potentially-significant relationship between continuing education and urban administration is explored by the author. The article begins with a review of the recent literature and concludes with a detailed description of an innovative curricular effort.

Sweet, David E. "Minnesota Metropolitan State College: A New Institution for New Students." Paper presented at the 21st annual Southern Regional Educational Board Legislation Work Conference, New Orleans, Louisiana, 21 July 1972. (ED 068 021)

Minnesota Metropolitan State College has recently been established as one of the few upper-level colleges (colleges offering only junior, senior, and graduate level courses) in the United States.

Torbet, William R. CREATING A COMMUNITY OF INQUIRY: CONFLICT, COLLABORATION, TRANSFORMATION. New Haven, Conn.: Harvard University, Graduate School of Education, 1973. (ED 103 551)

This publication concerns the experience of the author during two years (1966-68) as director of an Upward Bound program, which had and still has the goal of helping poverty high school students gain admission to college.

UNIVERSITY WITHOUT WALLS. HONOLULU MODEL CITIES. Mount Pleasant: Central Michigan University, 1974. (ED 108 308)

Central Michigan University has been operating an external degree program for the Honolulu Model Cities Program since February 1972. The Institute for Personal and Career Development (IPCD) is the component that extends the goals of the program--equal access to education for personal enrichment, career alternatives, and increased upward mobility--beyond the physical campus of the university.

Zarnowiecki, James, and Murphy, Thomas P. "University Without Walls." In
UNIVERSITIES IN THE URBAN CRISIS, edited by Thomas P. Murphy, pp. 241-58.
New York: Dunellen Publishing, 1975.

>The university without walls concept is a result of the university's
>response to students' needs. The Campus-Free College of the Dis-
>trict of Columbia is explained in this chapter. Problems relating
>to the doctoral world are illustrated in the Union Graduate School
>of the Union for Experimenting Colleges and Universities. Also
>considered are the problems in accrediting experimental programs
>and the implications for the future.

Section B

CITIZEN INVOLVEMENT IN URBAN PROBLEMS

Berry, Gordon L. "Education in the Inner-City Schools: The Community Challenge." JOURNAL OF BLACK STUDIES 3 (March 1973): 315-28.

Two of the major challenges facing urban schools today are: (1) the need to offer productive educational programs for an ever-changing student population, and (2) their ability to broaden the base of community participation in the operation of schools.

Crowe, M. Jay, and Smith, T. Michael. CITIZEN PARTICIPATION IN DENVER. Vol. 2. Denver: Denver Urban Observatory, 1972.

A detailed case study is reported of citizen participation efforts of volunteer target area resident groups in planned community change. The planning of a higher education center in downtown Denver was the focal point of the eighteen-month study.

Gow, Steels, and Salmon-Cox, Leslie. UNIVERSITY-URBAN INTERFACE PROGRAM. A UNIVERSITY AND ITS COMMUNITY CONFRONT PROBLEMS AND GOALS. Pittsburgh, Pa.: University of Pittsburgh, 1972. (ED 070 695)

This is a report on a series of university-community forums in the Goals Project of the University-Urban Interface Program of the University of Pittsburgh in which the relationships of urban universities and their urban communities are explored.

Harris, George Dewey, Jr. "A Study of Citizen Participation in the Educational Decision-Making Process as Perceived by Parents From A Lower Socio-Economic Neighborhood." Ph.D. dissertation, Michigan State University, 1970.

This study was designed to provide an understanding of the role of auxiliary personnel in the public school system. It focused on gathering ideas and perceptions of the functions of aides by the four levels of educators present in Richmond, Virginia. The study yields specific conclusions, but more importantly it provides recommendations and implications which include job descriptions and written guidelines as well as planning outlines for hiring, identifying job functions, and inservice programming.

Harris, J. John III, and Johnson, Leon, Jr. "A Theoretical Rationale: General Education Through an Urban Public Community College Can Promote Community Development." HIGH SCHOOL JOURNAL 58 (May 1975): 348-60.

McKay, Olive. "Community Involvement in the Solution of Urban Problems." ADULT LEADERSHIP 17 (September 1968): 107-8, 151-52.

> This is a report of the Northern Virginia Pilot Project in Community Education, an experiment funded by Title I of the Higher Education Act. The purpose of the project was to explore ways in which community leaders of a metropolitan area could be organized in a variety of programs which would better equip them to deal on their own with the many problems of an urban society.

Myers, Ernest R. THE ROLE OF COLLEGE-COMMUNITY RELATIONSHIPS IN URBAN HIGHER EDUCATION PHASE II--EXPLORATORY PLANNING. AN EXPLORATORY STUDY OF AN URBAN UNIVERSITY PROTOTYPE. Washington, D.C.: Federal City College, 1971. (ED 059 409)

> In 1968 Federal City College in Washington, D.C. was given funds to explore the role of college-community relationships in urban higher education. The present report relates the findings of this project's second phase, which was threefold: (1) to identify and explore various means for the college and the community to engage in joint urban problem-solving efforts, (2) to design and experiment with new instructional service delivery programs, methods and processes for improving college-community relations, and (3) to analyze the Federal Communication Commission's and, where possible, the community's needs and resources for improving reciprocal relationships.

Nehnevajsa, Jiri. UNIVERSITY-URBAN INTERFACE PROGRAM. PITTSBURGH GOALS AND FUTURES. Pittsburgh, Pa.: University of Pittsburgh, University-Urban Interface Program, 1973. (ED 073 039)

> Future community changes in Pittsburgh over the next five years are predicted in this study, the purpose of which is to determine the extent of community consensus regarding changes and the extent to which widely-differing perspectives of community leaders might contribute to conflict.

_____. "University-Urban Interface Program. Pittsburgh Goals: Notes on Metropolitanism." Paper presented at the Community-University Forum on Metropolitan Government, Pittsburgh, Pennsylvania, 24 February 1972. (ED 070 697)

> One of the priority areas for study in the University-Urban Interface Program at the University of Pittsburgh is community goals as they relate to metropolitan governance. This report includes some of the findings of the Pittsburgh Goals Study organized from data gathered through a questionnaire sent to key Pittsburgh community leaders.

Nehnevajsa, Jiri, and Brictson, Robert C. "University-Urban Interface Program. Pittsburgh Goals: Some Thoughts on Health Issues." Paper presented at the Community-University Forum on Health Problems, Pittsburgh, Pennsylvania, 9 December 1971.

> Comments from community leaders in Pittsburgh concerning health issues point out some of the major examples of the concerns and suggestions for action voiced in the University-Urban Interface Program study on Pittsburgh goals.

Paulson, Belden. "Urban Dilemma: Contributing Factors." JOURNAL OF EXTENSION 11 (Spring 1973): 15-22.

> This is a special urban issue, discussing trends and factors involved in urban crises. Paulson cites interrelationships between urban and rural areas, and urges comprehensive planning in urban projects.

Randolph, Harland A., et al. THE ROLE OF COLLEGE-COMMUNITY RELATIONSHIPS IN URBAN HIGHER EDUCATION. Vol. 1: PROJECT SUMMARY AND OVERVIEW. FINAL REPORT. Washington, D.C.: Federal City College, 1969. (ED 041 569)

> This report, the first of a three-volume study, presents the findings and conclusions of phase 1 of the Federal City College Research Project on the role of college-community relationships in urban higher education, planned as a four-phase study. This report presents the background of phase 1, the approach and methods used, and the principal findings of the study, all of which concern the nature of the relationships and social processes involved.

Randolph, Harland L., and Reid, Lorenzo E. "College-Community Planning in the Nation's Capitol." CATHOLIC EDUCATION REVIEW 67 (November 1969): 162-72.

> Formation of, and cooperation between, college and community organizations to achieve the most favorable impact of an urban college upon the surrounding populace are two of the highlights of this article.

Schwebel, Andrew I., et al. "University Extension in Urban Neighborhoods: A New Approach." JOURNAL OF HIGHER EDUCATION 47 (March-April 1976): 205-15.

> This essay describes the conceptualization and development of a pilot urban-extension program designed to enhance community self-help efforts while assisting the university in its educational, research, and service functions.

Seyffert, M. Gordon. "The University as an Urban Neighbor." In UNIVERSITIES IN THE URBAN CRISIS, edited by Thomas P. Murphy, pp. 137-59. New York: Dunellen Publishing, 1975.

The university is in the process of becoming an integral part of the urban community. There are many problems involved in this process, particularly the suspicion of the residents. Suggestions are given for managing neighborhood relations and the impact of university expansion is explored.

THE URBAN UNIVERSITY AND THE URBAN COMMUNITY. 6 vols. Boston, Mass.: Boston University Metrocenter, 1966. (ED 025 692)

These volumes contain the results of six seminars conducted at Boston University during 1966. They focused upon the urban university and its environment, education for metropolitan living, the urban university and community action, problems of town and gown, and a look at the future of the university.

Van Dusen, Albert C., and Brictson, Robert C. "University-Urban Interface: Issues, Methodology, Prospects." Paper presented at the annual meeting of Eastern Psychological Association, Boston, Massachusetts, 27-29 April 1972. (ED 072 717)

The University-Urban Interface Program of the University of Pittsburgh is an action-research effort designed to study the actual and potential roles of the university in the community in a time of change.

Section C
PROGRAMS FOR URBAN MINORITIES

Association of University Evening Colleges. PROCEEDINGS OF THE 30TH AN-
NUAL MEETING. San Francisco, Calif.: n.p., 1968.

> In this annual convention the emphasis was on the universities' proper
> urban-extension role and responsibility in the inner city, and on
> steps toward greater flexibility and wider educational opportunities
> in higher continuing education.

Banyon, Shelia Doran. INTENSIVE PROGRAMMING FOR SLOW LEARNERS.
Columbus, Ohio: Charles E. Merrill Publishing Co., 1968.

> This book is designed to present in necessary detail a short-term,
> intensive program for a group of young children with learning dis-
> orders.

Barth, Roland S. "The University and Urban Education." PHI DELTA KAPPAN
51 (September 1969): 36-40.

Bell, Peter. BASIC TEACHING FOR SLOW LEARNERS. London: Garden City
Press, 1970.

> This book presents some basic teaching techniques used in England
> to help the slow learner.

Berdow, John Richard. "The Development of the Adult Education Programs in
Three Selected Institutions in St. Louis, Missouri: A Comparison." Ed.D. dissertation, Indiana University, 1968.

> The growth patterns of adult education programs in three universi-
> ties were compared with regard to origin, purpose, expansion, sup-
> port, student and teacher personnel, and determination of programs.

Brazziel, William F. "New Urban Colleges for the Seventies." JOURNAL OF
HIGHER EDUCATION 44 (March 1970): 169-78.

Urban land-grant colleges should be established to bring minority groups into the college-trained work force.

Carioti, Frank V., ed. A COLLEGE GROWS IN THE INNER-CITY. New York: Educational Facilities Laboratories, 1967. (ED 026 820)

A brief history of the development of the Detroit Institute of Technology centers on already existing buildings acquired by the institute. The present situation is discussed in terms of the resources available to an inner-city student, the types and number of students served, and the presently adapted facilities--that is, assignable gross space and space utilization.

THE CHURCH, THE UNIVERSITY AND URBAN SOCIETY. New York: National Council of Churches of Christ, 1972. (ED 076 165)

This document presents the report of a project designed to examine the relationship of higher education to urban society and to develop purposes and programs that the churches, community groups, institutions of higher education, and other organizations may pursue so that higher education in its various forms can be more responsive to the critical needs of urban life.

Colmen, Joseph G., and Wheeler, Barbara A., eds. HUMAN USES OF THE UNIVERSITY: PLANNING A CURRICULUM IN URBAN AND ETHNIC AFFAIRS AT COLUMBIA UNIVERSITY. New York: Columbia University, Urban Center, 1970. (ED 049 348)

This curriculum planning project of the Columbia University Urban Center attempts to provide Columbia University with a complete profile on current and planned curricula dealing with urban and minority affairs, to recommend directions for the university's future development to order these recommendations according to priority, and to outline structural arrangements and strategies to facilitate their implementation.

Cory, Genevieve Hansen. "The Relationship Between Televised Instruction and Cognitive Performance, Attitude Change, and Self-Reported Behavior Change in Sub-Groups With Varying Backgrounds and Characteristics." Ph.D. dissertation, University of California, 1972.

In this study, a consumer-education program was structured for open broadcast television, with viewing-discussion groups set up among disadvantaged adults. These were analyzed by the subgroup characteristics of race, education, age, and income as well as by attitudes of liking for previous school experience and liking for commercial television.

Coyle, H. F., Jr., et al. PROJECT TOTAL--TO TEACH ALL: AN INQUIRY INTO THE DEVELOPMENT OF A MODEL FOR IDENTIFYING UNMET NEEDS

IN URBAN POST SECONDARY EDUCATIONAL OFFERINGS. FINAL REPORT.
Akron, Ohio: Akron University, Center for Urban Studies, 1973. (ED 092 779)

> Using the Akron metropolitan area as the study area, the explora-
> tory research of Project Total--To Teach All--is aimed at develop-
> ing a generalizable model for analyzing urban adult educational
> needs, with disadvantaged adults receiving special attention. A
> primary purpose of the Project Total study is the collection of data
> for use in planning and coordinating post secondary programs serv-
> ing the needs of the urban disadvantaged.

Daly, Kenneth, ed. INSTITUTIONS OF HIGHER EDUCATION AND URBAN
PROBLEMS: A BIBLIOGRAPHY AND REVIEW FOR PLANNERS. Monticello,
Ill.: Council of Planning Librarians, 1973.

> The demand that institutions of higher education do something about
> the problems of the cities generated a great deal of discussion dur-
> ing the 1960s. Unrest within the university and in the city pro-
> voked a number of programs and projects that attempted to bring
> the resources of the university to bear on different aspects of ur-
> ban life, and even sometimes to make these resources available to
> city-dwellers.

Eland, Calvin. THE CULTURALLY DISADVANTAGED: A FIELD EXPERIENCE
GUIDE. MATERIALS/ONE. Washington, D.C.: American Association of Colleges for Teacher Education, 1968. (ED 080 497)

> This guide resulted from the work of fourteen colleges and universi-
> ties participating in the Red River Valley Inter-Institutional Project,
> which related to the education of the culturally-disadvantaged child.
> The project included two field experiences, one urban and the other
> rural, as well as orientation meetings and discussions.

Ellwood, Caroline. SURVEY OF UNIVERSITY ADULT EDUCATION IN THE
METROPOLITAN AREA OF NEW YORK. New York: New York University,
School of Continuing and Extension Services, 1967. (ED 013 405)

> This survey of university-level adult credit and noncredit courses
> covers over thirty colleges and universities in greater New York--
> largely evening colleges, community colleges, and community ser-
> vice programs.

Evans, Arthur H., Jr. INTERINSTITUTIONAL COOPERATION IN THE URBAN
CITY: SOME HYPOTHESES AND A CASE STUDY. San Francisco: City College of San Francisco, 1968. (ED 037 215)

> The San Francisco Consortium, composed of the University of Cali-
> fornia Medical Center, University of San Francisco, San Fran-
> cisco State College, Golden Gate College, and City College of
> San Francisco, is based on geographic proximity rather than on the
> similarity of goals among member institutions. The author of this

study has made several statements, or hypotheses, about the nature of interinstitutional programs and has used the San Francisco Consortium as a case study against which to test and highlight each statement.

Fahrer, Kimberly, and Vivolo, Robert, eds. ERIC REFERENCES ON URBAN AND MINORITY EDUCATION. EQUAL OPPORTUNITY REVIEW. New York: Columbia University, ERIC Clearinghouse on the Urban Disadvantaged, 1976. (ED 128 492)

Two hundred and twenty-four items comprise this guide to the literature on urban and minority education not easily accessible to educational researchers, decision makers, and practitioners. It brings together significant works in this area which appear in the January 1975 through April 1976 issues of RESOURCES IN EDUCATION.

Ferman, Louis A. DISADVANTAGED YOUTH: PROBLEMS OF JOB PLACEMENT, JOB CREATION AND JOB DEVELOPMENT. Manpower Administration, U.S. Department of Labor. Ann Arbor: University of Michigan, 1967.

The purpose of this report is to review and assess the impact of selected strategies in job placement, job creation, and job development.

Ferver, Jack C. "Needed: An Urban Extension Service." ADULT LEADERSHIP 18 (January 1970): 210-12, 223-28.

The author's position is that Title I of the Higher Education Act of 1965 has demonstrated that institutions of higher education can make an important contribution to the solution of community problems. But there are limitations, the greatest of which are the lack of adequate program funds and the mounting program needs.

FIRST ANNUAL REPORT OF THE TEMPLE UNIVERSITY NEIGHBORHOOD EXTENSION PROGRAM. Philadelphia, Pa.: Temple University, Division of Vocational Education, 1972. (ED 101 039)

The primary purposes of this program are: (1) to develop a new concept of Adult Basic Education at inner-city neighborhood centers, (2) to develop program offerings around the expressed needs and interests of participants, and (3) to identify next-step opportunities for graduating students.

Gains, Lynette S. "Teaching in the City: A Need for Reeducation." CONFERENCE COURSE READING UNIVERSITY OF PITTSBURGH 25 (July 1969): 33-44.

Getschman, M. L. "An Introductory Home Economics Curriculum for the Intermediate EMH Child." A team project presented to Dr. Louise Smith. De Kalb: Northern Illinois University, 1968.

This is a good beginning in the field of EMH (educable mentally handicapped). It presents curriculum for intermediate levels for both boys and girls in grooming, learning to work in the kitchen, and manners for eating out. These plans would be a part of the EMH classroom activity.

Gipson, Betty Kennedy. "Legal Problems of Low-Income Families With Suggestions for Teaching in High School Home Economics." ILLINOIS TEACHER 12 (Winter 1968-69): 139-80.

Goldberg, Miriam. "Factors Affecting Educational Attainment in Depressed Urban Areas." In EDUCATION OF THE DISADVANTAGED: A BOOK OF READINGS, edited by A. Harry Passow, pp. 31-61. New York: Teachers College Press, 1967.

Disadvantaged students have few learning experiences that prepare them for either intellectual or attitude learning. The author points out that disadvantaged students can't handle abstractions and discusses how they rebel seeking status and protection outside in the streets.

Goldstein, Bernard. LOW INCOME YOUTH IN URBAN AREAS. New York: Holt, Rinehart and Winston, 1967.

Research studies and child psychology theories are incorporated into this factual report on low-income youth in urban areas. A thorough analysis of these youth from work practices to leisure time activities is presented.

Goodfriend, Harvey J., et al. CENTRE CITY COMMUNITY COLLEGE--A SIMULATION IN COMPREHENSIVE PLANNING. San Diego, Calif.: San Diego State College, 1969. (ED 031 056)

A simulation of a community college in an urban setting is presented to test certain hypotheses and to accumulate ideas showing the ways in which planning can become more comprehensive and successful.

Goodrich, Andrew. "Minority Group Programs in Community/Junior Colleges." SOCIAL EDUCATION 36 (February 1972): 120-24.

_____. "A Survey of Selected Community Services Programs for the Disadvantaged at Inner-City Community Colleges." Ph.D. dissertation, University of Michigan, 1969. (ED 046 366)

This study investigates community-service programs for the disadvantaged at inner-city community colleges in order to construct a descriptive history of the various programs' origins, development, and essential components.

Greenberg, Gilda M. "An Approach to Teaching a Course: Psychology of the Disadvantaged." ADULT LEADERSHIP 20 (March 1972): 317-18.

Greenberg developed a classroom learning atmosphere that allowed
the students to interact and express their feelings and attitudes
about the disadvantaged. From this experience, each student developed a project based on working with an inner-city student,
youth center, or recreational facility. Through this project, the
link between theory and application was made more effective.

Hartman, Eugene L. A COMPARISON OF SELECTED TRANSFER STUDENTS
WITH A MATCHED POPULATION. Columbia: University of Missouri, 1968.
(ED 023 383)

Junior college transfers chosen from three colleges of the University
of Missouri were compared with native students at the end of their
junior year using as criteria, (1) the size of the high school graduating class, (2) high school rank, (3) sex, (4) age at college entrance, and (5) the college of the university chosen for the junior
year.

Hinchliff, William E. "Urban Problems and Higher Education: Federal City
College." WILSON LIBRARY BULLETIN 43 (February 1969), 527-33.

Hough, Olga B. "Students Help the Elderly Urban Poor." WHAT'S NEW IN
HOME ECONOMICS? 51 (October 1969): 19.

This is a proposal to prepare students to understand and help the
urban poor. It has implications for students at the junior high
school level.

Jenkins, Martin D. THE URBAN AFFAIRS PROGRAMS OF HIGHER EDUCATION
ASSOCIATIONS: WHAT THEY ARE DOING AND WHAT THEY CAN DO.
Washington, D.C.: American Council on Education, 1971. (ED 069 236)

The purposes of this study were to ascertain the degree of sensi-
tivity that associations of higher education have to the involvement
of colleges and universities in urban affairs, and to encourage the
associations to give increased attention to the urban involvement
of their members in their programs and activities.

Jenkins, Martin D., and Ross, Bernard H. "The Urban Involvement of Higher
Education." JOURNAL OF HIGHER EDUCATION 46 (July-August 1976):
399-407.

In response to growing unrest in urban areas during the 60's, colleges and universities began expanding their urban activities.
This article utilizes data from a nationwide survey to analyze
selected trends and issues in higher education urban involvement
by focusing on the current status and future direction of urban
affairs activities on college and university campuses.

Klotsche, J. Martin. THE URBAN UNIVERSITY--AND THE FUTURE OF OUR
CITIES. New York: Harper and Row, 1966.

Urban universities now enroll nearly one-half of the students in degree-granting institutions. Because of this increasing trend, these urban universities are becoming an integral part of their respective communities. The major portion of the volume discusses aspects of the school-community relationship. The final chapter presents the problems which an urban culture imposes on an urban university and the responses necessary for coping with them successfully.

Kopelke, Phyllis B., and Kock, Moses S. "A Community College Perspective on New Careers." JUNIOR COLLEGE JOURNAL 41 (June-July 1971): 14-16.

The Early Childhood Education Program at Essex Community College is used as a model to present the intentions, realizations, and disappointments of a new careers program for inner-city adult residents.

Kroepsch, Robert H., and Thompson, Ian M., comps. URBAN AND MINORITY CENTERED PROGRAMS IN WESTERN COLLEGES AND UNIVERSITIES, 1969-1970. Boulder, Colo.: Western Interstate Commission for Higher Education, 1969. (ED 034 645)

Based on a survey of more than 160 colleges and universities in thirteen western states, this report examines the programs which have been developed by institutions of higher learning to meet the various needs of minority groups and urban centers.

Lash, John S., et al. TEXAS SOUTHERN UNIVERSITY: FROM SEPARATION TO SPECIAL DESIGNATION. Houston: Texas Southern University, 1975. (ED 111 305)

Texas Southern University was created in a decisive period of racial turmoil in national affairs, a period which eventually resulted in dramatic and far-reaching changes in legal and societal accommodations of the ambitions and aspirations of minority people. This monograph is a summary and analysis of the history of this institution.

"Lincoln Land: A College on the Move." COMMUNITY COLLEGE FRONTIERS 3 (Spring 1975): 28-31.

Lincoln Land Community College (Springfield, Illinois) serves a population with a mixture of industrial, agricultural, and commercial interests in a geographical area of 3,420 square miles. This article describes its special programs for the blind, the placement of its graduates, and some of its programs and problems.

Long, Huey B. "Cape Kennedy: Launching Pad for the Urban Agent Concept." ADULT LEADERSHIP 16 (September 1967): 94, 108.

Under a grant from the Ford Foundation and funds provided by Title I of the Higher Education Act, this urban agent concept was utilized in developing projects to meet the needs of public administrators and community service organizations.

Mansfield, Ralph. ANNUAL PLANNING CONFERENCE. Chicago, Ill.: Chicago City College, 1967. (ED 021 538)

This planning conference was convened at Chicago City College (CCC) in 1967 for the purposes of (1) developing a forward-looking approach to the multiple problems of social, political, and economic origin in the urban complex as they relate to the community college, (2) planning various ways in which CCC can prepare to meet the changing needs of urban education tasks in the 1968-80 era, and (3) encouraging better student, faculty, and administration performances required for a more effective education.

Mayer, Martin. "Higher Education for All? The Case of Open Admissions." In UNIVERSITIES IN THE URBAN CRISIS, edited by Thomas P. Murphy, pp. 215-39. New York: Dunellen Publishing, 1975.

In 1969 the Board of Higher Education of New York City, the controlling body of City University, began a number of studies looking toward the day when the university would undertake to accept all graduates of the city's high schools, regardless of their performance in high school or their achievement on examinations. This chapter explains how the formula for entrance was established and how the program has progressed.

Meyers, Trienah. "The Extra Cost of Being Poor." JOURNAL OF HOME ECONOMICS 62 (June 1970): 379-84.

This article discusses the economic factors involved in being poor. Teaching the poor to stock up on foods when on sale, or to take advantage of out-of-season sales, is not possible for these people. They have immediate needs that must be taken care of. They do not have enough money to prepare for the future, too, as we can.

Moore, E. Maynard. "Visitation to Selected Urban Community Colleges, Spring-Summer 1973. Report of Internship presented to Union Graduate School." Ph.D. dissertation, Union Graduate School, 1973. (ED 104 465)

To secure a broader perspective on possible community-service programs at Central YMCA Community College (Illinois), and to observe and confirm some of the national trends in postsecondary education, a series of field visits to nine private and six public urban oriented two-year colleges were made during the spring and summer of 1973.

Morton, Richard K. "Education for Urban Living." IMPROVING COLLEGE AND UNIVERSITY TEACHING 19 (Fall 1971): 263-66.

This article concerns itself with preparation for urban living. The author emphasizes that education today must be directed toward modern urbanism, the globalization of relationships, and human concerns. The nature of the urban society is described as pluralistic, changing, and conflicting. The need for education to address the areas of housing conflicts, rapid population mobility, economic and employment inequalities, and societal goal setting. The use of education as the vehicle for fulfilling human potential is discussed at length.

Nash, George, and Waldorf, Dan. THE UNIVERSITY AND THE CITY. FINAL REPORT. Washington, D.C.: Bureau of Social Science Research, 1971. (ED 059 694)

This study presents individual in-depth case studies that focus on the efforts of nine diverse institutions of higher education which work with urban problems that exist in their areas.

O'Sullivan, Maurice J., et al. DYNAMICS, ROLE, AND FUNCTION IN INTER-UNIVERSITY COLLABORATION. FINAL REPORT. Bridgeport, Conn.: Higher Education Center for Urban Studies, 1972. (ED 068 044)

The Higher Education Center for Urban Studies was formed as a consortium in 1968 by five institutions of higher education located in or near Bridgeport, Connecticut. It has been involved mainly in urban research, community service, and in facilitating educational services for disadvantaged people. This report is a study made to determine whether or not HECUS should continue the present course and nature of its operations, or should redirect them.

Paige, Joseph C. "4-H for Central City Minorities." JOURNAL OF EXTENSION 8 (Spring 1970): 11-16.

This is an article about a program offered by the only urban land-grant college, Federal City College in Washington, D.C. The author discusses 4-H with children of poor ethnic groups in the District of Columbia.

Palola, Ernest G., and Oswald, Arthur R. URBAN MULTI-UNIT COMMUNITY COLLEGES: ADAPTATION FOR THE '70'S. Berkeley: University of California, Center for Research and Development in Higher Education, 1973. (ED 068 096)

This study examines the relationship between the organizational structure of multiunit community college districts and the performance of urban campuses in serving disadvantaged students. Emphasis is on the expanding functions and changing structure of urban community colleges, the relationship between district office and district colleges, and problems and constraints involved in programing for "new" community college students.

Parsons, Jerry. "Inner-City Youth Programs: Guidelines." JOURNAL OF EXTENSION 9 (Summer 1971): 31-40.

The author suggests program and organizational guidelines for the

professional youth leader to use in developing and implementing
4-H programs in the inner city.

Passow, A. Harry, ed.   OPENING OPPORTUNITIES FOR DISADVANTAGED
LEARNERS.   New York: Teachers College Press, 1972.

Paulson, Belden.   "Research, Training, and Action in Milwaukee's Inner Core:
A Case Study About Process."   ADULT LEADERSHIP 15 (April 1967): 361-62,
384-87.

> This is a report of a project conducted by the University of Wis-
> consin-Milwaukee and the University of Wisconsin Extension to
> make university resources relevant to particular needs of the sur-
> rounding urban community.

Peelle, Carolyn Curtiss.   "A New Design for Higher Education: The UMASS Center
for Urban Education."   PHI DELTA KAPPAN 56 (April 1975): 399-402.

> The question of the capability of institutions of higher education
> to solve major problems in public education is addressed.   The es-
> tablishment of the Center for Urban Education is discussed with a
> profile of its achievements resulting from efforts attempting to solve
> the problems of public education.   The design of the center is dis-
> cussed not only as a prototype for education but for other profes-
> sional fields.   Ultimately the center idea can provide a responsive
> vehicle in higher education for local school systems and communi-
> ties to effect desired educational changes.

Perlman, Daniel H.   A BRIEF HISTORY OF ROOSEVELT UNIVERSITY.   Chicago,
Ill.: Roosevelt University, 1972.   (ED 076 115)

> Perlman traces the history of this institution since its founding in 1945.

Porte, Michael.   "The Mission of Urban Communication."   "Teaching Communication in a Business Orientation Program for Black Students."   Two papers
presented at the Action Caucus of the 58th annual meeting of the Speech Communication Association, Chicago, Illinois, 27-30 December 1972.   (ED 084 596)

> A speech communication department in an urban college should per-
> form functions geared to the special requirements of urban students
> and their communities.   The second paper presents in some detail a
> special business communication course developed for potential man-
> agement trainees, all of them black, selected by a major manufac-
> turing firm.

PRELIMINARY REPORT OF THE COMMITTEE ON THE UNIVERSITY AND THE
CITY.   Cambridge, Mass.: Harvard University, 1968.   (ED 027 827)

> In May 1968, a committee was appointed at Harvard to evaluate
> the university's effort to help both the community and the nation find solu-

tions to urban distress, poverty, economic imbalance, racial ine-
quality, and disease. The committee was charged with recommend-
ing new actions, if necessary, and determining the role Harvard
should play in responding to urban issues both as a center of learning and as an urban institution.

Ramo, Roberta Cooper. URBAN LEGAL PROCESS: DEVELOPMENT OF ORIGI-
NAL COURSE MATERIALS TO TEACH LEGAL PROBLEM-SOLVING SKILLS AND
KNOWLEDGE TO UNDERGRADUATES IN THE URBAN SCIENCES. FINAL RE-
PORT. Raleigh, N.C.: Shaw University, 1970. (ED 061 921)

The present document presents an outline and discussion of a course
designed to instruct students in the workings of the legal processes
as related to the solving of today's urban problems. The project
in its entirety created a product that can be adapted to meet the
needs of urban science students from several instructional points of
view.

A REPORT ON SIX SEMINARS TO ASSIST IN PLANNING A HIGH RISE, HIGH
DENSITY URBAN CAMPUS FOR MANHATTAN COMMUNITY COLLEGE. New
York: Caudill, Rowlett, and Scott, 1968. (ED 027 881)

The problem discussed in this publication was to create, on 4.5
acres of Lower Manhattan, a junior college to meet the needs of
11,000 full- and part-time students as well as the surrounding urban community.

Roberts, Thomas Bradford. "Middle Class Values--Opinions Differ." TODAY'S
EDUCATION 59 (January 1970): 20-23.

The article delivers two opinions on middle-class values, both very
much in support of them but in different ways and for different reasons.

Samuels, Frank. "ABE Urban Extension: Towards a Strategy of Intervention."
ADULT LEADERSHIP 24 (October 1975): 68-70.

The author feels that ABE urban extension presents one approach to
the solution of the educational problems of the urban disadvantaged.
In order for this to work, the institutional climate must be such that
the student must be viewed as legitimate when compared to other
students enrolled in the community college.

Sawyer, G. M. "One University's Urban Commitment." JOURNAL OF EX-
TENSION 11 (Spring 1973): 41-48.

In this special urban issue, Sawyer presents a revised paper read
at Opening Convocation, Texas Southern University, Houston, Texas,
21 September 1972.

Simmons, Ron. AN ALTERNATIVE CURRICULUM MODEL FOR URBAN EDUCA-
TION AND COMMUNITY AFFAIRS PROGRAMS IN HIGHER EDUCATION.
WORKING PAPER NO. 103. Wayne, N.J.: William Paterson College, De-
partment of Urban Education and Community Affairs, 1973. (ED 088 873)

> This document describes the urban education program at William
> Paterson College of New Jersey. Urban education is defined as
> educating people for living and coping with an urban environment,
> including politics, crime and drug prevention, and delivery of ser-
> vices to cities.

Sturdivant, Frederick D. THE GHETTO MARKETPLACE. New York: Free Press,
1969.

> What this book attempts to do is to bring together the views of schol-
> ars, government officials, politicians, writers from the business press,
> and other writers who have studied various elements of this problem.
> It is hoped that this collection and the rather detailed bibliography
> will lead to further research and corrective action.

Tillman, Sheadrick A. "Focus on the Urban Community." ILLINOIS CAREER
EDUCATION JOURNAL 31 (Spring 1974): 20-32.

> The conception of an occupational education delivery system for an
> institution located in an urban community was realized at Chicago
> State University through changes in administrative structure and
> curriculum, an interdisciplinary faculty approach, a contemporary
> cooperative work-experience program, and a cooperative urban
> teacher-education program.

U. S. Congress. Senate. Select Committee on Equal Educational Opportunity.
EQUAL EDUCATIONAL OPPORTUNITY. HEARINGS ON PART 12--COMPEN-
SATORY EDUCATION AND OTHER ALTERNATIVES IN URBAN SCHOOLS.
92d Cong., 1st sess., 1971.

> The Senate Select Committee on Equal Educational Opportunity held
> hearings on quality in urban education on 14 July 1971. The lengthy
> testimony of various educators and professors is given with discus-
> sion of problems peculiar to integrated urban areas.

UNIVERSITY OF MAINE URBAN ADULT LEARNING CENTER FOR THE MODEL
NEIGHBORHOOD IN PORTLAND, MAINE; FINAL REPORT: PHASE II, FOR
THE FISCAL YEAR ENDED JUNE 30, 1972. Portland: University of Maine,
1972. (ED 101 146)

> The Urban Adult Learning Center's (UALC) primary goal is to im-
> prove and expand the educational and employment opportunities for
> all residents in the Portland Model Cities target area who are six-
> teen years of age or older and who have not reached the eighth-
> grade educational level. The phase two foundation section reviews
> historical background and goals of the project.

URBAN AFFAIRS ACTIVITIES SPONSORED BY COLLEGES AND UNIVERSITIES: AN INVENTORY OF CURRICULA, RESEARCH AND EXTENSION IN THE BALTIMORE REGION. Baltimore, Md.: Regional Planning Council, 1967.

> From the twenty-four institutions of higher learning in the Baltimore region, twenty report one or more activities in the field of urban affairs. In all, about 350 activities were reported.

THE URBAN UNIVERSITY AND THE URBAN COMMUNITY. 6 vols. Boston: Boston University Metrocenter, 1966. (ED 025 692)

> A series of six seminars, conducted by Boston University Metrocenter from 9 March to 31 May 1966, covered the following topics: "The Urban University and Its Environment," "Education for Metropolitan Living," "The Urban University and Community Action," "Problems of Town and Gown," "The Urban University and the Arts," and "University and City: A Look to the Future."

Wargo, Michael J., et al. FURTHER EXAMINATION OF EXEMPLARY PROGRAMS FOR EDUCATING DISADVANTAGED CHILDREN. Palo Alto, Calif.: American Institute for Research, 1971.

> The study was the third in a series that had as its primary objective the identification and description of successful compensatory education programs for precollege disadvantaged children.

Wilson, Gerald L., and Doederlein, Arthur P. "Speech Communication as Survival Training: The C.H.A.N.C.E. Program." SPEECH TEACHER 22 (September 1973): 189-95.

> The essay describes a program at Northern Illinois University which teaches communication skills in order to aid minority students in surviving the college curriculum.

Worley, A. Douglas, and Einbecker, Polly Godwin. "A Plan to Improve the Organization Structure of Pensacola Junior College to Meet Educational Needs of Under-Educated Adults in the Regional Community." Ed.D. dissertation, Nova University, 1974.

> Data concerning race, income level, age, employment status, and education were identified for each census tract in the Pensacola Junior College area. On the basis of this data, census tracts were combined into compatible neighborhoods and an organizational approach was designed to bring educational and community services into twenty-two educationally-disadvantaged urban neighborhoods.

Ziffern, Abbie. "The Urban Agent Program of the Urban Studies Center." ADULT LEADERSHIP 18 (October 1969): 107, 122-23.

> Rutgers University has sponsored a small cadre of volunteer urban

agents. In addition to doing community work, each agent partici-
pates in an informal get-together with other agents from all over
the state and in an urban issues seminar. The program serves as a
link between the university and the urban community.

Section D
STAFF TRAINING FOR URBAN EDUCATION

ADULT BASIC EDUCATION TEACHER TRAINING INSTITUTE: PROBLEMS OF
THE URBAN POOR, PARTICULARLY THE URBAN POOR WHITE. Berkeley,
Calif.: Wright Institute, 1971. (ED 101 120)

> The focus of a two-week summer institute for seventy-seven Adult
> Basic Education (ABE) teachers, administrators, and counselors from
> the western United States, Hawaii, and Alaska, was on the prob-
> lems of the urban poor, with emphasis on the urban poor white.
> Major emphasis was placed on nonlearning problems of the urban
> poor.

Baptiste, Hansom P., Jr., and Meindl, Carmelita O. AN ANSWER TO A CHAL-
LENGE, INNOVATION IN UNIVERSITY CURRICULUM. South Bend: University of Indiana, 1971. (ED 062 932)

> This paper discusses the development, implementation, and evalua-
> tion of a first-year action program at Indiana University, South
> Bend, designed to prepare urban people for careers in education.
> The program was initiated because of the need presented by the
> ever-growing concentration of blacks in the urban environment who,
> in many cases, face poor housing, unemployment, and no political
> identity.

Bernert, Roman A. "Teacher Education and a Model Cities Project." MAR-
QUETTE UNIVERSITY EDUCATION REVIEW 2 (Fall 1971): 47-55.

Bess, Lorraine J., et al. URBAN ON-SITE TEACHER EDUCATION PREPARA-
TION IN TEACHER EDUCATION CENTERS: BRUCE ELEMENTARY SCHOOL,
SEATON ELEMENTARY SCHOOL, TRUESDELL ELEMENTARY SCHOOL. Wash-
ington, D.C.: District of Columbia Teachers College, 1971. (ED 077 916)

> This paper presents an inner-city, elementary teacher-education pro-
> gram which focused upon (1) the acquisition of teaching techniques
> and skills in the urban learning setting, (2) the learning of theory
> together with reinforced practice in functional field experiences,
> (3) the reinforcement of principles of child growth and develop-

ment through direct contact with the children, (4) the development of procedures for individualized instruction and diagnostic teaching, and (5) the encouragement of continuous evaluation.

Best, Gilmary. CORD CONDUCTS A FEASIBILITY STUDY. FINAL REPORT. Detroit: Marygrove College, 1972. (ED 070 418)

The objectives of the study were to: (1) design a plan for reeducating certified urban teachers in multicultural dimensions, (2) obtain the cooperation of key personnel in the surrounding school districts, (3) design a credit and sharing plan by which personnel and facilities of each of the colleges would be pooled as sources of the learning array, and (4) recruit certified teachers from the above school systems. The design for a complete institute for reeducating certified urban teachers in multicultural dimensions is included in the report.

Bowman, Garda, and Klopk, Gordon J. NEW CAREERS AND ROLES IN THE AMERICAN SCHOOL. New York: Bank Street College of Education for the Office of Economic Opportunity, 1968.

The study attempts to explore the whole range of educational roles and functions in two ways: (1) inductively, through the development, coordination, and analysis of fifteen demonstration programs in the training and collaborative utilization of professionals and nonprofessionals, and (2) deductively, through consultation with outstanding educators and with experts from related disciplines.

Buck, Benjamin. THE INTRODUCTORY URBAN EDUCATION PROGRAM. Mankato, Minn.: Mankato State College, School of Education, 1971. (ED 065 480)

Mankato State College's introductory Urban Education Program provides students with an intercultural, interdisciplinary, and interinstitutional educational program.

CAREER OPPORTUNITIES PROGRAM. Farmington: University of Maine, 1973. (ED 085 390)

The Career Opportunity Program (COP) selected trainees from a group of low-income, model neighborhood people generally conceded to be high-risk college material. This was done in order to provide an example of the "multiple entry routes" to the teaching profession.

Ciminillo, Lewis M. "Problems and Opportunities At An Urban Campus: A Professional Semester in Secondary Education." COLLEGE STUDENT JOURNAL 9 (April 1975): 135-40.

Indiana University Northwest is placing a substantial part of its teacher education program in the schools and communities where its students eventually will be employed. The professional semester is a competency-based program organized into a number of modules each of which is planned to develop a different skill.

Claye, Clifton M. PREPARING TEACHERS FOR THE INNER-CITY. Cedar Falls: University of Northern Iowa, 1968. (ED 024 638)

> Improvements of teacher preparation programs discussed in this book include (1) recruiting students who have demonstrated some degree of scholastic excellence, (2) designing a number of participation and observation activities for prospective teachers, and (3) structuring these activities to correlate with course content.

Cody, George Thomas. "Student-Teacher Effectiveness Comparing the University of Michigan School of Education, Urban Education, and General Teacher Training Programs." Ph.D. dissertation, University of Michigan, 1973.

> A means for assessing the human quality in school management systems was considered. The results indicate an approach to bridge the gap between instructional design and implementation as well as management of the educational enterprise.

Comeaux, Pamela Harris. A FOLLOW-UP STUDY OF 1967-1970 COOPERATIVE URBAN TEACHER EDUCATION GRADUATES. Kansas City, Mo.: Mid-Continent Regional Educational Laboratory, 1971. (ED 100 925)

> The Cooperative Urban Teacher Education (CUTE) program enrolled 295 volunteer teachers in their senior year of college and trained them for one semester in an inner-city school. Data indicated that a significantly greater proportion of the graduates of the CUTE program teach in inner-city schools and plan to teach in the inner-city schools in the future as compared to graduates who did not go through the program.

Cudlipp, Katherine Y. "Teaching Veterans to Teach." CHANGE 4 (March 1972): 13-14.

> This program is aimed at training black veterans to teach in inner-city elementary schools.

DeNevi, Don. "The Mission Rebels as Trainers of Teachers." PEABODY JOURNAL OF EDUCATION 47 (March 1970): 286-89.

> A unique program is presented here which is intended to provide urban teachers with the necessary training to meet the needs of their students.

DiPasquale, Vincent C. THE GARY-INDIANA-MOORHEAD STATE COLLEGE PROJECT IN COOPERATIVE URBAN TEACHER PREPARATION. Gary, Ind.: Gary City Public School System; Minnesota: Moorhead State College, 1972. (ED 073 091)

> The various aspects of the program discussed in this report are: travel allowance, tuition and costs, housing and cooperating schools, rationale and assumptions, objectives of the program, description of

the project, themes of the GIMSC (Gary-Indiana-Moorhead State College Project) curriculum, project evaluation, and limitations of the project.

DIRECTOR'S EVALUATION OF URBAN INSTRUCTIONAL TRAINING AND DEVELOPMENT INSTITUTE, ESSEX COUNTY COLLEGE. Newark, N.J.: Essex County College, 1971. (ED 077 910)

This is a second-year report on a program to train college graduates for community college teaching functions with low-income and urban minority students.

Dixon, Billy Ray. "A Curriculum for an Introduction to Urban Education." Ed.D. dissertation, University of Massachusetts, 1973.

This study reviews the phenomenon of inner-city education in which educators are predominantly white and unfamiliar with ghetto life. The introduction of curricula content into teacher education has been based on research and developed expertise. This study makes recommendations relative to developing courses for teachers who work in ghetto settings. These recommendations are specific to the issue, and extrapolate possible impact of such training.

Drake, Thelbert L., and Thompson, Diane D. INFLUENTIALS UPON STUDENT TEACHERS IN THREE PRE-SERVICE SETTINGS. Storrs: University of Connecticut, 1971. (ED 083 205)

This study was done to determine if the influence of key individuals on student teachers differed by preservice teaching settings and if such persons could affect differences in the perceived beliefs and behaviors of student teachers towards their pupils and towards teaching. Sixty student teachers were divided into three groups for the project.

DUALITY IN SOCIETY: DUALITY IN TEACHER EDUCATION. Chicago: Northeastern Illinois University, 1971. (ED 074 016)

Northeastern Illinois University developed a student teaching program designed to prepare the student teacher to function in both an inner-city setting where children are less advantaged socioeconomically as well as in an outer-city setting where children come from relatively higher socioeconomic backgrounds. The five major aspects of the program include cross assignment, group counseling, seminars, other backup experiences, and duality workshops.

Eble, Kenneth. "Among School Children." ENGLISH EDUCATION 1 (Fall 1969): 18-28.

A university English department head comments on his teaching experience at a junior high school and on subsequent changes made in the university's English curriculum, including methods used to prepare teachers for the public schools.

Egerton, John. "Central Missouri's Inner City Project Tells a Near-Parable." SOUTHERN EDUCATION REPORT 2 (May 1967): 26-31. (ED 026 339)

In response to a challenge by the Kansas City Public Schools superintendent, Central Missouri State College instituted the Inner City Teacher Education Project to prepare teachers to work with disadvantaged children.

Ellis, Charles. "Career Education and Culture." ILLINOIS CAREER EDUCATION JOURNAL 30 (Spring 1973): 17-20.

Implications for teacher education in preparing teachers for inner city schools are discussed here.

AN EXPERIMENTAL PROJECT FOR ADMINISTRATIVE TRAINEES. New York: Camp Fire Girls, 1969.

The objective of the project was to explore the practicability of a program of noncredit college study and work experience to prepare mature women, including noncollege graduates, for administrative positions with social service agencies.

Fisher, Francis D. AN IMPRESSION OF 'THE OAKLAND PROJECT'--CONSIDERATIONS IMPORTANT TO THE DESIGN PROJECTS LINKING UNIVERSITIES AND CITY GOVERNMENT. Washington, D.C.: Urban Institute, 1972. (ED 071 612)

For five years graduate students in the Oakland Project of the University of California at Berkeley have been working at jobs in the city of Oakland while continuing their studies. This paper describes the Oakland Project and seeks to extract from it considerations important to the design of any university-city relationship.

Fox, Arthur Douglas. "A Study of a University Program to Prepare Minority Urban Education Administrators." Ed.D. dissertation, University of Colorado, 1976.

This study documents and analyzes the project development processes to assess the perceived effectiveness in recruiting and developing black educators for urban school leadership positions. The main findings were that recruitment was effective, and that students showed progress in personal growth and administrative skills.

Gold, Milton J. "Programs for the Disadvantaged at Hunter College." PHI DELTA KAPPAN 48 (March 1967): 365.

The programs offered by Hunter College in New York City for training teachers of the disadvantaged are described. Hunter offers (1) specialized training courses, (2) programs for teachers of Puerto Rican children, and (3) various National Defense Education Act institutes.

Hall, Betty, and Levine, Daniel U. UNDERSTANDING METROPOLITAN LIVING: DESCRIPTION AND EVALUATION OF A COOPERATIVE CITY--SUBURBAN PROGRAM FOR URBAN STUDENTS IN THE 1970'S. SUMMER PROGRESS REPORT. Kansas City: University of Missouri-Kansas City, Center for the Study of Metropolitan Problems in Education, 1970.

> Understanding Metropolitan Living was a cooperative summer school sponsored and conducted by a suburban school district in Johnson County, Kansas, and the central city school districts in Kansas City, Kansas, and Kansas City, Missouri.

Haubrich, Vernon F. "Teachers for Big City Schools." Lecture given at Teachers College, New York, N.Y., 27 January 1970. (ED 038 438)

> The social-psychological bases of programs to prepare teachers for disadvantaged youth are as important to the eventual success of the program as any technique or lesson plan which seems to be momentarily fruitful. In view of the predicted oversupply of teachers, the school system must try to select teachers who will function best in the classroom, be able to see their role as teachers instead of as functionaries, and give a long period of service to teaching.

Horton, George R. "VTR Brings Inner City to IE Majors." AMERICAN VOCATIONAL JOURNAL 44 (September 1969): 59-60.

> This is a report from the Industrial Education Department at Bowling Green State University which is pioneering the use of professional quality videotape recordings to enrich field experiences that precede student teaching in the professional sequence for education majors.

Ikeda, K., et al. "Program Profile: A 7-Year Program to Prepare Talented Youths for College." URBAN REVIEW 5 (June 1972): 41-45.

> The article discusses the decisions made in the development of a precollege program to provide special educational opportunities to talented youths who, because of limiting economic and social forces, would not normally enter college or earn degrees.

AN INNER CITY COLLEGE-COMMUNITY TEACHER EDUCATION PROGRAM. Washington, D.C.: Entry for the American Association of Colleges for Teacher Education, 1972 Distinguished Achievement Award, 1972.

> This report describes the development of an inner-city college-community teacher education program designed at Mount St. Mary's College in Los Angeles, California.

AN INSTITUTE FOR TEACHERS AND TEACHER-TRAINERS IN ADULT BASIC EDUCATION OF URBAN ADULTS: FINAL REPORT. Jefferson City, Mo.: Lincoln University, 1972. (ED 099 633)

Katz, William A. "The Poor: A Problem of Priority. An Interview With Dr. Doxey A. Wilkerson." EQUAL OPPORTUNITY REVIEW, March 1973. New York: Columbia University, National Center for Research and Information on Equal Educational Opportunity, 1973. (ED 085 428)

> This is the first issue of EQUAL OPPORTUNITY REVIEW, a publi-
> cation to provide opinion and information to educators and laymen in
> furthering equal educational opportunities in our society. In this issue
> Dr. Wilkerson, a professor of education at Jeshiva University who
> is mainly involved with the preparation of teachers for effectively
> working with children of the poor, was interviewed.

Klopf, Gordon J., and Bowman, Garda M. TEACHER EDUCATION IN A SO-CIAL CONTEXT: A STUDY OF THE PREPARATION OF SCHOOL PERSONNEL FOR WORKING WITH DISADVANTAGED CHILDREN AND YOUTH. New York: Bank Street College of Education by Mental Health Materials Center, 1966.

> The purposes of the study were to describe selected programs designed
> to improve the knowledge, skills, and attitudes of school personnel
> for working with disadvantaged children and youth, to identify unique
> and significant elements of such programs, and to develop basic
> concepts and guidelines for emerging programs of this type.

Krosky, Roy T. "The Inner City Teacher Education Program." A report submit-ted to the American Association of Colleges for Teacher Education, September 1971. (ED 067 378)

> The Inner City Teacher Education Program designed by the Univer-
> sity of Northern Colorado, emphasizes the preparation of prospec-
> tive teachers for working in urban schools whose populations are
> composed of children from culturally-diverse backgrounds.

Leinwand, Gerald. "Needed: A College of Public Education and Service." SOCIAL EDUCATION 34 (March 1970): 305-10.

> This is a concrete description of the components and operation of
> an institution based on a new pattern of teacher education and
> responsive to community needs, and one which the author envisions
> as the logical next step in urban higher education.

Leonard, George E., et al. THE DEVELOPMENTAL CAREER GUIDANCE PROJ-ECT: AN INTERIM REPORT. Detroit: Wayne State University, 1968.

> This report covers the objectives of the Developmental Career Guid-
> ance Project which are: (1) to aid a selected group of inner-city
> high school students to raise and broaden their educational and occu-

pational aspirations, (2) to develop a pilot program designed to better meet the needs of inner-city youth, (3) to involve the staffs of the participating schools in the program, and (4) to systematically evaluate the program.

Levine, Daniel U. "Urban Teacher Training." In UNIVERSITIES IN THE URBAN CRISIS, edited by Thomas P. Murphy, pp. 259-84. New York: Dunellen Publishing, 1975.

This chapter attempts to identify the elements of a good urban teacher-training program. In addition the author describes several special programs that exemplify some or all of these elements.

Lutz, Frank. "Problems in Training and Utilizing Urban Education Leadership." Paper presented at the annual convention of the American Association of School Administrators, Dallas, Texas, 21 February 1975. (ED 109 737)

The positions expressed reflect several perspectives on the university-urban district cooperative leadership program carried out by Pennsylvania State University and the Philadelphia school district. Statements are made by students now holding positions as high school assistant principal, elementary principal, elementary assistant principal, administrative assistant to the district superintendent, and special program director.

Mann, Philip H., ed. MAINSTREAM SPECIAL EDUCATION: ISSUES AND PERSPECTIVES IN URBAN CENTERS. Coral Gables, Fla.: Miami University, 1974. (ED 093 141)

Provided are nineteen presentations made to 200 participants in a conference on issues of mainstreaming, career education, and teacher education programs for urban, handicapped children.

Massey, Walter E., and Eschenbacher, Herman F. "Training Science Teachers for the Inner City: The ICTOS Program at Brown University." PHYSICS TEACHER 10 (February 1972): 80-85.

The program is described in terms of science and education components. Science background is provided in specially-designed basic courses in the various disciplines with advanced courses selected in one chosen area. In-school activities are stressed beginning in the sophomore year.

A MODEL PROGRAM FOR IMPROVING THE EDUCATION OF PRESERVICE AND INSERVICE TEACHERS OF ELEMENTARY, SECONDARY AND EXCEPTIONAL CHILDREN IN METROPOLITAN AREAS: INTERIM REPORT. Storrs: Connecticut University, School of Education, 1968. (ED 026 290)

This report describes the procedures to date (staffing, housing, testing, operation of the education program, and the inservice program for public school personnel), evaluation (including student, cooperating inservice personnel, and outside evaluations), and anticipated modifications.

Monroe, George E. REPORT OF AN URBAN EDUCATION REFORM EXPERIMENT: PROBLEMS AND PROMISE. PART I. PROJECT DEVELOPMENT. SUPPLEMENT TO FINAL REPORT OF THE 5TH CYCLE TEACHER CORPS PROJECT. Chicago: Illinois University, Chicago Circle Campus, 1972. (ED 087 745)

> The Fifth Cycle Teacher Corps Project was undertaken by the University of Illinois at Chicago Circle to (1) fulfill a stated mission of a university especially created to help resolve urban problems, (2) find effective ways to help an inner-city community utilize its own resources, and (3) conduct research on the effective uses of evaluation in educational reform projects.

Moore, E. Maynard, ed. "The Campus and the City: A Symposium." Report of symposium held in Chicago, Illinois, 10 March 1973. (ED 104 466)

> This symposium was planned to provide a format for Ph.D. candidates in the Union Graduate School who wished to join with leaders in higher education in an open discussion of current issues in urban higher education.

Mungo, Samuel J., and Durham, Joseph T. "From Cornfield to Ghetto: Training of Disadvantaged Teachers for the So-Called Disadvantaged." ILLINOIS SCHOOL JOURNAL 53 (Spring-Summer 1973): 3-9.

> This article describes the purpose and operation of the Illinois State University Urban Education Program, an innovative, community-based program designed for teacher trainees planning to teach in urban secondary schools. Some student reactions are included.

Murphy, Thomas P., ed. "Minority Faculty Recruitment." In his UNIVERSITIES IN THE URBAN CRISIS, pp. 325-51. New York: Dunellen Publishing, 1975.

> Areas explored in this chapter are: the need for minority faculty, supply barriers to recruitment, sex discrimination, and affirmative action programs.

Obradovic, Sylvia M. COURSE EVALUATION OF THE WAYNE STATE UNIVERSITY "AUGUST 24-28, 1964 WORKSHOP FOR 71 TEACHERS NEWLY ASSIGNED TO 20 DETROIT SCHOOLS." Detroit: Wayne State University, 1966.

> A one-week workshop preceding assignment to inner-city schools was evaluated through in-depth interviews of fifty-two out of seventy-one participants after completion of their first year of teaching. An outside investigator conducted the interviews, using a forty-eight-item questionnaire covering reactions to the workshop, reactions to the first semester of teaching, and general recommendations for future workshops.

Ornstein, Allan C. METHODS FOR CONDUCTING TEACHER BEHAVIOR RE-
SEARCH: WITH IMPLICATIONS FOR TEACHERS OF THE DISADVANTAGED.
Ph.D. dissertation, New York University, 1970. (ED 046 863)

> This paper is primarily based on the "Conceptual Framework," in
> SELECTED TEACHER BEHAVIOR ATTITUDES RATED AS DESIRABLE
> BY NINTH-GRADE DISADVANTAGED STUDENTS AND NINTH-
> GRADE TEACHERS OF THE DISADVANTAGED. The author con-
> siders both the current status of such research and the fact that
> the problem is so complex that no one knows or can agree upon
> the definition of a competent teacher. In an attempt to improve
> this situation, twenty-seven recommendations for future research
> are listed.

Otten, Jane, ed. AN EXPERIMENT IN PLANNED CHANGE: THE URBAN
TEACHER EDUCATION PLANNING GRANT PROGRAM OF THE AMERICAN
ASSOCIATION OF STATE COLLEGES AND UNIVERSITIES. Skokie, Ill.: Sears-
Roebuck Foundation, 1973. (ED 079 270)

> The American Association of State Colleges and Universities in con-
> junction with the Sears-Roebuck Foundation offered financial sup-
> port to various state colleges and universities which were planning
> innovative programs for educating inner-city teachers.

Otto, Henry J., and Bessent, Wailand. EVALUATION OF AN EXPERIENCED
TEACHER FELLOWSHIP PROGRAM. Austin: Texas University, 1970. (ED 051
077)

> This book describes and evaluates a twelve-month postgraduate pro-
> gram to develop better leadership in urban elementary schools in
> disadvantaged neighborhoods.

Pamerantz, Phillip. AN INSTITUTE TO PREPARE LOCAL URBAN ADULT BASIC
EDUCATION ADMINISTRATORS AND TEACHERS TO BECOME ABE TEACHER
TRAINERS: JUNE 1, 1971-MAY 1, 1972. FINAL REPORT. Bridgeport, Conn.:
University of Bridgeport, 1972. (ED 101 194)

> The twelve-month federally-funded project at the University of
> Bridgeport, Connecticut, was designed to prepare adult basic edu-
> cation (ABE) administrators and teachers (serving urban Puerto Ricans,
> blacks, and whites) to become teacher trainers. Focus was on build-
> ing a multiregional teacher capability in ABE through teacher train-
> ing models.

Peelle, Carolyn Curtiss. "A New Design for Higher Education: The UMass
Center for Urban Education." PHI DELTA KAPPAN 56 (February 1975): 399-402.

> The Center for Urban Education proposes that higher education be-
> come an agent for change that works closely with local schools and
> communities. Emphasis is placed on curricula for diverse popula-
> tions, inservice training, upward mobility, career training, and
> dialogues between diverse cultures and different races.

PROCEEDINGS OF THE ANNUAL MEETING OF THE WESTERN ASSOCIATION OF GRADUATE SCHOOLS. The 11th meeting, Las Vegas, Nevada, 24 March 1969. Pocatello: Idaho State University, 1969. (ED 059 686)

> This is the report of the 1969 annual conference of the Western Association of Graduate Schools. The first general meeting held at the conference presented three speeches by minority students from the area graduate schools. Discussed in these addresses were the problems confronting American Indian, Mexican American, and black students in the schools.

Reed, George N. PREPARATION OF TEACHERS FOR SCHOOLS OF THE INNER CITY. Cedar Falls: University of Northern Iowa, 1968.

A REPORT TO THE FACULTY FOR THE OFFICE OF INSTRUCTION. FOREST PARK COMMUNITY COLLEGE. St. Louis, Mo.: St. Louis Junior College District, 1975. (ED 116 762)

> This annual report indicates the status of each department and division at Forest Park Community College, a predominantly black inner-city two-year college in St. Louis, Missouri.

Rippey, Robert M. REPORT OF AN URBAN EDUCATION REFORM EXPERIMENT: PROBLEMS AND PROMISES. SECTION II: PROJECT EVALUATION. SUPPLEMENT TO THE FINAL REPORT OF THE 5TH CYCLE TEACHER CORPS PROJECT. Chicago: University of Illinois, Chicago Circle Campus, 1972. (ED 087 746)

> This document recounts the efforts of an urban college of education (the one at the University of Illinois, Chicago Circle) to develop a cooperative program in urban teacher education. It deals with the origin of the project, operational problems encountered, solutions attempted, and critical functions of systematic evaluation. Also included are statements of conclusion by the development coordinator.

Rivlin, Harry N. THE URBAN EDUCATION PROGRAMS AT FORDHAM UNIVERSITY'S SCHOOL OF EDUCATION. Bronx, N.Y.: Fordham University, School of Education, 1968. (ED 025 481)

> The preparation programs for urban teacher, administrator, and specialist (e.g., guidance counselor, school social worker, etc.) at Fordham University's School of Education are described in terms of the urban setting, the university-community relationship, cooperation between the school of education and other university units, and the faculty involved, including the name of each member and a brief description of his qualifications.

Ross, Calvin, and Swick, Kevin. "An Explanatory Study in the Development of Positive Changes in Student-Teacher Attitudes Toward Inner City Teaching."

EDUCATION AND URBAN SOCIETY 2 (November 1969): 112-17.

This is a report of the Purdue University student-teacher opinionnaire.

Rouse, Robert, and Rouse, Virginia. INNOVATIVE METHODS TRAIN TEACHERS AT INDIANA UNIVERSITY. Bloomington: Indiana University, 1974. (ED 095 178)

This paper describes an individualized program of teacher training at Indiana University. Student teachers are able to choose their own teaching experience from several projects. The Shawnee Project gives novice teachers the opportunity to cope with inner-city school problems in real situations.

Sarbaugh, L. E. "What Should be the Unique Role of Teaching or the Unique Applications of Teaching in Departments of Speech Communication Located in Urban Environments?" Paper presented at the annual meeting of the Speech Communication Association, New York, New York, 8 November 1973. (ED 084 586)

Schwartz, Henrietta S., and McCampbell, James. "Staff Development in Low Power Transactional Organizations: The Administration of an Experimental Program in Urban Education." Paper presented at the annual meeting of the American Educational Research Association, Chicago, Illinois, April 1974. (ED 091 486)

This paper examines the management of training programs for educators who are or will be working in inner-city schools.

Sobel, Max A., and Maletsky, Evan M. TEACHING MATHEMATICS TO THE SLOW LEARNER IN THE INNER CITY SCHOOLS. Upper Montclair, N.J.: Montclair State College, 1972. (ED 076 515)

The 1972 Distinguished Achievement Award Entry from Montclair State College, Montclair, New Jersey, focuses on the preparation of secondary mathematics teachers for slow learners in the inner city. Twenty students participated in the three-week field experience program. The first week consisted of on-campus seminars which explored teaching methods appropriate for the motivation of slow learners and developed sample classroom teaching units and materials. The next two weeks were spent doing field work in five different inner-city schools.

"Specialized Teacher Training for Inner City Schools." SCHOOL AND SOCIETY 100 (April 1972): 214-15.

This article describes fine programs being developed in various colleges throughout the nation, funded by Sears and Roebuck. This financial grant permits these colleges to plan new nontraditional programs for teachers of minority groups or inner-city children.

Stevenson, William W., et al. UPDATING THE PROCESS AND CONTENT OF TEACHER EDUCATION COURSES TO REACH LESS ADVANTAGED ADULTS IN METROPOLITAN AREAS. FINAL REPORT. Stillwater: Oklahoma State Department of Vocational and Technical Education and Oklahoma State University, 1970. (ED 049 191)

> A two-week institute was held to orient participants to the world of the disadvantaged and to give them ideas on methods of training teachers to work with disadvantaged adults. The seventy-seven participants (including teacher educators, teachers, community workers, personnel of the Oklahoma State Department of Education and counselors) attended lectures by consultants from the School of Occupational and Adult Education at Oklahoma State University, the Oklahoma State Department of Vocational and Technical Education, and the Area Manpower Institutes for Development of Staff, and participated in small-group discussions. An important feature of the institute was a live-in arrangement whereby participants spent four nights in the home of a disadvantaged family. Most participants evaluated the institute favorably. In addition, a four-month follow-up found that most participants subsequently engaged in one or more activities designed to improve education for the disadvantaged. The report includes lists of participants and consultants, a schedule of daily activities, and some of the evaluation forms developed.

STUDENT EXCHANGE PROGRAM. Washington, D.C.: Teachers College; Brockport, N.Y.: University of New York-Brockport, 1969. (ED 037 418)

> This paper describes the origin and development of a student exchange program between the State University College at Brockport, New York, and the District of Columbia Teachers College in Washington, D.C. Preceded by an exchange of professors from the respective laboratory schools in 1966-67 and operated without financial grants of any kind, the program now offers senior-year student teachers the opportunity to teach and live in environments with which they have previously had little contact.

SUMMARY OF THE ADULT BASIC EDUCATION INSTITUTE FOR TEACHERS AND TEACHER-TRAINERS OF URBAN ADULT POPULATIONS. Pt.1. 26 July-6 August 1971. Washington, D.C.: Howard University, 1971. (ED 099 670)

> This document begins with an overview, emphasizing characteristics of the institute participants. A background section focuses on the status of American, urban-dwelling blacks, the population group with which the teachers will be working. Eleven speeches are presented to familiarize participants with the relationships between color and sex and income, schooling, and employment, and to acquaint them with community resources, the importance of the political process, and the ways reading and mathematical skills can assist students in their social and economic lives.

SUMMARY OF THE ADULT BASIC EDUCATION INSTITUTE FOR TEACHERS AND TEACHER-TRAINERS OF URBAN ADULT POPULATIONS. Pt. 2. 26 July 1971-31 August 1972. Washington, D.C.: Howard University, 1972. (ED 099 671)

Contrary to the statement in the title, part 2 of the summary of institute proceedings is concerned with the period from 7 August 1971 to 31 August 1972. It reports the results of an opinionnaire taken the last day institute participants were assembled at Howard University, and the uses to which the participants put their institute experience after they returned to their places of work.

Talmage, Harriet, and Monroe, George E. "The Teacher as a Teacher Educator." EDUCATIONAL LEADERSHIP 27 (March 1970): 609-13.

The Cooperative Program in Urban Teacher Education (CPUTE) is discussed in this article. It is an experimental program in the College of Education, University of Chicago. The background of the program is presented as well as its goals. The discussion emphasizes that any teacher program should be a regenerative system which maintains the functioning of the education process.

TEACHER CORPS--URBAN. CYCLE II, FINAL PROGRAM REPORT. Los Angeles: University of Southern California, 1969. (ED 042 689)

This document reports the Cycle II Teacher Corps Urban Program at the University of Southern California, a two-year effort to prepare teachers to work effectively in disadvantaged communities of diverse racial and ethnic groups including blacks, Mexican Americans, poor whites, Japanese, Koreans, and Samoans.

TEACHER TRAINING CONFERENCE: ADULT BASIC EDUCATION FOR URBAN CLIENTS. FINAL REPORT. Chicago: University of Chicago, 1972. (ED 061 489)

The University of Chicago's Teacher Training Conference provided for an examination of opinion and research from the field of adult basic education, practice in skill development and application, an experience of an urban community, and encounters which centered on personal, political, and educational ideology.

URBAN ADULT BASIC EDUCATION SPECIAL TEACHER TRAINING INSTITUTE. FINAL REPORT. Los Angeles: Pepperdine University, Center for Urban Affairs, 1972. (ED 101 122)

The report covers the activities, data, and data analysis of the institute. The institute was directed to 100 teachers and supervisors of adult basic education (ABE) in regions eight, nine, and ten to acquaint them with the needs and problems of black urban adults.

URBAN EDUCATION INSTITUTE. DIRECTOR'S REPORT, 1970-1971. Pasadena, Calif.: Pasadena City College, 1971. (ED 077 912)

This is an interim report on the Urban Education Institute, which is designed to provide part-time inservice education for experienced community college personnel.

Vance, Irvin E. MSUIC-MP MICHIGAN STATE UNIVERSITY INNER CITY MATHEMATICS PROJECT. East Lansing: Michigan State University, 1970. (ED 038 325)

The project's objectives are to provide inservice training for teachers in inner-city schools; to train critic teachers, supervisors, and other personnel for inner-city schools in mathematics; to prepare undergraduate and graduate students to teach in inner-city schools; to establish a program which reaches inner-city students at an early age; and, to establish an undergraduate program which will provide mathematics and science teachers for inner-city students.

Walsh, Huber M. THE LANGUAGE STUDY: AN EFFORT TOWARD MORE MEANINGFUL PREPARATION FOR PRESERVICE ELEMENTARY TEACHERS IN THE INNER CITY. St. Louis: University of Missouri-St. Louis, 1968. (ED 025 479)

The Off-Campus Methods Course was devised to relate theories of methods courses to actual teaching experience. There are three episodes divided into four phases. The first phase is theoretically based on teaching strategies, the second phase demonstrates these strategies, the third phase applies these to a microteaching situation, and the fourth phase analyzes the microteaching phase.

THE WEST DALLAS TEACHER EDUCATION PROGRAM. Denton: North Texas State University, 1975. (ED 117 096)

This program is a competency-based program to better prepare teachers for service in inner-city schools. The program utilizes a field-based, professional semester format to directly relate instruction and clinical practice.

Winter, J. Alan, and Mills, Edgar W. RELATIONSHIPS AMONG THE ACTIVITIES AND ATTITUDES OF CHRISTIAN CLERGYMEN: A PRELIMINARY REPORT. New York: National Council of Churches of Christ, 1968.

This is a report on the Research on Training for Metropolitan Ministry project. RTMM has two main objectives: to increase understanding of the relationships between the attitudes, skills, and activities of clergymen, and to identify changes in these aspects after training.

Wolfe, Alan. "Working With The Working Class." CHANGE 4 (February 1972): 48-53.

This describes teaching experiences in an experimental college where students are members of ethnic minority groups and parents have low socioeconomic backgrounds.

Woodbury, John Carr. "The Development of the Center for Urban Education."
Ed.D. dissertation, University of Massachusetts, 1970.

> This study provides an analysis of the Center for Urban Education
> (CUE) at the University of Massachusetts during 1968-1970. The focus
> is related to the potential for teacher-training institutions to effect
> change in urban schools. The necessary components for viable ur-
> ban center development and the ability of a university to promote
> a relevant program is discussed. This dissertation provides some in-
> sight into this area of concern: How can a predominantly white
> educational institution solve problems in urban and largely black
> America?

Yee, Albert H. "What Should Modern, Urban Society Expect of Teacher Education?" EDUCATION IN URBAN SOCIETY 2 (May 1970): 277-94.

> Yee proposes that a systems-management point of view be taken in re-
> vising present teacher-education programs.

Zauderer, Donald G. URBAN INTERNSHIPS IN HIGHER EDUCATION. Washington, D.C.: ERIC Clearinghouse on Higher Education, 1973. (ED 085 039)

> This monograph is primarily for faculty members and administrators
> in colleges and universities, as well as intern directors in nonedu-
> cational institutions to assist them in formulating judgments about
> the design and implementation of internship programs.

Part III

ADULT EDUCATION

Any society which experiences even moderate change within the single lifetime of its people must make some formal or informal provision for the education of its adult population. New knowledge, understanding, and skills are required by adults to accommodate change successfully if the society's vigor is to be maintained.

So it is that adult education is universal and has, in fact, a substantial genealogy in the United States which records the systematic efforts of individuals, groups, and institutions to provide useful learning experiences for adults from all walks of life. However, there has been until recent years a curious failure to note the compatibility of the terms education and learning. Education was somehow viewed as the property and function of schools. Learning by children and youths in schools was education, learning by adults through organized but nonschool activities was something else, and not considered particularly important to educators.

Adult education as a field of professional study and practice is relatively new and has become significant because of emerging demands in this rapidly changing society for the adult population to accommodate a world for which they were not socialized.

The forces of new technology, affluence, and social expectation that were unleashed in the 1960s brought greater attention to the need for adults to learn and, subsequently, for people and resources that could organize and facilitate adult-oriented learning activities. How to teach adults, where to teach them, when to teach them, and what to teach them, became the questions for professional adult educators to ask and for which they seek still to provide satisfactory answers.

Part 3 opens with the problem of financing since no single institutional structure supports adult education in ways comparable to the public provisions for elementary and secondary schools, colleges, and universities. Adults as voluntary students pose special problems for educators. Attracting adults to educational programs and maintaining their participation often is a struggle for organizers along with the development of appropriate content material directed to a diversity of interests and at a wide range of achievement levels. Characteristically there has been little communication or coordination among purveyors of adult education but, as the number of professional adult educators grows, so too does awareness of the need for synergy among those who function in behalf of the adults and their need to learn.

Section A

FINANCES

Griffith, William S., et al. PUBLIC POLICY IN FINANCING BASIC EDUCATION FOR ADULTS: AN INVESTIGATION OF THE COST-BENEFIT RELATIONSHIPS IN ADULT BASIC EDUCATION IN PUBLIC SCHOOLS AND COMMUNITY COLLEGES. Vol. 1: SUMMARY AND RECOMMENDATIONS. Chicago: University of Chicago, Department of Education, 1974. (ED 099 638)

> This volume reports the study's two purposes: to document the effects of federal financing of adult basic education on the delivery systems at the state and community levels for both general adult and adult basic education, and to propose models for coordinating adult education which might optimize the extent and variety of adult education offerings for the public.

_____. PUBLIC POLICY IN FINANCING BASIC EDUCATION FOR ADULTS: AN INVESTIGATION OF THE COST-BENEFIT RELATIONSHIPS IN ADULT BASIC EDUCATION IN PUBLIC SCHOOLS AND COMMUNITY COLLEGES. Vol. 2: STUDY DESIGN AND FINDINGS. Chicago: University of Chicago, Department of Education, 1974. (ED 099 639)

> This volume presents the study's two purposes (to document the effects of federal financing of adult basic education on the delivery systems, and to propose models for financing adult education) and describes its design and findings in detail. It is a complete account of the project, including descriptions of case studies in each of five states.

_____. PUBLIC POLICY IN FINANCING BASIC EDUCATION FOR ADULTS: AN INVESTIGATION OF THE COST-BENEFIT RELATIONSHIPS IN ADULT BASIC EDUCATION IN PUBLIC SCHOOLS AND COMMUNITY COLLEGES. Vol. 3: COMMUNITY CASE STUDIES. Chicago: University of Chicago, Department of Education, 1974. (ED 099 640)

> This volume presents community case studies of cities selected for the study. Cities were examined in such major areas as historical development, program, enrollments and courses, financing, impact of federal funds, teaching staff, and salaries.

Finances

Lang, Carroll L. "Community Education in the Los Angeles Metropolitan Area." COMMUNITY EDUCATION JOURNAL 3 (January 1973): 10-13.

> This article surveys the nature of community education in the Los Angeles area and examines specific programs in the area. Needs for community education are discussed, and the future of community education is examined.

Mezirow, Jack, et al. LAST GAMBLE ON EDUCATION DYNAMICS OF ADULT BASIC EDUCATION. Washington, D.C.: Adult Education Association of the U.S.A., 1975. (ED 112 119)

> This publication reports the result of a two-year research project on urban adult basic education (ABE). It develops comprehensive and analytical descriptions of significant aspects in the ABE program operation and classroom interaction, and the perspectives of those involved. The study was conducted in large-city public schools throughout the country, and the information gathered is presented in chapter form, following an introduction stating methodology and rationale.

Roberts, Markley. "Pre-Apprenticeship Training for Disadvantaged Youth: A Cost-Benefit Study of Training by Project Build in Washington, D.C." Ph.D. thesis, American University, 1970.

> This study focuses on the benefits and costs of preapprenticeship institutional training aimed at reducing the employment problems of male inner-city black youths.

STAFF STUDY ON COST AND TRAINING EFFECTIVENESS OF PROPOSED TRAINING SYSTEMS. Orlando, Fla.: Naval Training Equipment Center, 1972. (ED 070 271)

> This study began the development and initial testing of a method for predicting cost and training effectiveness of proposed training programs. A prototype training-effectiveness and cost-effectiveness prediction model was developed and tested.

Section B

PARTICIPATION AND RECRUITMENT

Bruker, R. M., and Talina, L. H. "Profile and Perceptions of the Part-Time Student." COLLEGE STUDENT SURVEY 4 (1970): 31-32.

> This study surveyed the profile and perceptions of the part-time student at the Edwardsville campus of Southern Illinois University. The report concludes with suggestions to overcome the students' negative feelings about their status.

CONTINUATION OF A SPECIAL EXPERIMENTAL DEMONSTRATION PROJECT IN ADULT EDUCATION. FINAL REPORT. Detroit: Detroit Public Schools, 1971. (ED 101 150)

> The project attempted to involve uneducated and undereducated and/ or unemployed and underemployed young adults in an education-tutorial-employment-oriented program. The report discusses the result of a review of the project's efforts and suggests changes where needed to achieve sound and humane urban-oriented educational practices.

Dobbs, Ralph C. "Ghetto Students' Expressed Reasons for Attending Formal Classes." COLLEGE STUDENT JOURNAL 6 (November-December 1972): 27-29.

> The investigator was able to name three factors which describe why adult students pursue continuing education classes: (1) personal educational-economic factor; (2) personal self-development factor; and (3) personal convenience.

Hawkins, Dorothy Lee. "A Study of Dropouts in an Adult Basic Education Program and a General Education Development Program and Suggestions for Improving the Holding Power of These Programs." Ed.D. dissertation, Indiana University, 1968.

> This investigation sought to discover why adults dropped out of the Adult Basic Education Program and the General Education Development Program in the New Orleans public schools, and to suggest ways of reducing the number of dropouts. A specially-constructed

interview schedule was used to obtain data from a 10 percent random sample of 1965–67 dropouts listed in the two programs.

Jack, Robert Lee. "A Survey Analysis of the Clientele of an Adult Basic Education Program for Welfare Recipients." Ed.D. dissertation, Indiana University, 1969.

Using a sample of fifty students completing the program and fifty program dropouts, all black women, this study investigated personal and participant characteristics of 1,307 Chicago welfare recipients who had been students in the Hilliard Adult Education Center during 1965 to 1968.

Lewis, Gerda Johanna. "A Study of Citizen Participation of Urban Renewal and Its Relationship to Adult Education." Ph.D. dissertation, Cornell University, 1957.

This study assessed the importance of citizen participation in urban renewal, examined and described current problems of citizen participation, and determined the role of public adult education in assisting with citizen participation in urban renewal.

Miller, Harry L. PATTERNS OF EDUCATIONAL USE OF A TELEVISED PUBLIC AFFAIRS PROGRAM. A STUDY OF METROPOLIS--CREATOR OR DESTROYER. New York: New York University, 1966. (ED 010 545)

A national survey with a case-study approach was undertaken to determine the educational outcomes of broadcasting a public affairs, educational television (ETV) program. This ETV program, a series of films and supplementary materials on the problems, dilemmas, and promise of modern urban life, was designed and televised in an effort to improve understanding of urban problems among educators and to stimulate the development of innovative urban education projects for adults.

Murtaugh, Leonard Paul. "Participation in Adult Education Programs and Attitudes Toward Public Schools." Ed.D. dissertation, Michigan State University, 1968.

Using a population of adults enrolled in 1967 in the 1,123 classes of the Flint, Michigan adult education program, this study examined the relationship between participation in these programs and the formation of changing attitudes toward public schools.

Nesbitt, Charles. "Designing Relevant Programs for Urban Black Adults." ADULT LEADERSHIP 22 (January 1974): 249-52.

The author describes a program which is designed to attract and hold significant numbers of urban black adults.

Passett, Barry, and Parker, Glenn M. "The Poor Bring Adult Education to the Ghetto." ADULT LEADERSHIP 16 (March 1968): 326-28, 348.

This is a report of a demonstration project to train 24 poor people, people who were unemployed or on welfare, to provide educational experience to more than 700 adults living in six urban ghettoes of New Jersey. The project was designed to: (1) develop new career opportunities for nonprofessionals, (2) test new methods of bringing adult education to ghettoes, and (3) test the capability of three training resources.

Robinson, Russell D. "Adult Education Participation in the Industrial Suburb of West Milwaukee, Wisconsin." ADULT EDUCATION 20 (Summer 1970): 226-32.

This community was studied to determine the availability and participation of adults in adult education programs. Although funds and facilities were available to support educational programs, the study revealed a low participation rate.

Sackett, Duane Harry. "A Descriptive Analysis of the Evening and Off-Campus Population, Temple University, Fall Semester, 1966-1967." Ed.D. dissertation, Temple University, 1967.

This study sought to: (1) describe the total population of the evening and off-campus divisions of Temple University, (2) identify evening and off-campus students' educational needs, and (3) suggest better means for servicing the needs of these students.

Seaman, Don F. PREVENTING DROPOUTS IN ADULT BASIC EDUCATION. RESEARCH TO PRACTICE SERIES. Tallahassee: Florida State University, Department of Adult Education, 1971. (ED 079 592)

Reasons given by adult basic education (ABE) students for leaving the program are interpreted and discussed, and implications for the ABE program are suggested. The reasons are classified in four categories: environment, physiology, wants and goals, and past experiences.

Shultz, John Stevenson. "A Comparative Study of Day and Evening Undergraduate Students in Temple University School of Business Administration." Ed.D. dissertation, Temple University, 1966.

A comparative study was made of the day and evening undergraduate students in the Temple University School of Business Administration. Pre- and post-tests were given and data accumulated on ten educational and personal factors with performance of each class analyzed in terms of these factors.

Totten, W. Fred. THE POWER OF COMMUNITY EDUCATION. Midland, Mich.: Pendell Publishing, 1970.

Participation and Recruitment

In this book, the innovator of the community school program in Flint, Michigan describes the experiences of participants in that program. Some of the topics discussed include the impact of the program on the solution of social problems, its effects on the prevention and control of crime and delinquency, and individual cases of growth and development.

Section C

CURRICULUM DEVELOPMENT

ABE IN THE INNER CITY PROJECT: INNOVATIVE PRACTICES STUDY. FI-
NAL REPORT, 1970-1971. New York: Columbia University, Center for Adult
Education, 1971. (ED 101 135)

> In its second year the project had two principal goals: (1) to ex-
> tend the first year's findings with a study of selected innovative
> practices in a large variety of urban adult basic education (ABE)
> programs, and (2) to disseminate findings of the project's first two
> years to urban ABE directors and selected professors of adult edu-
> cation.

Briggs, Larry, et al. MOTT FOUNDATION PROJECTS MOTT PROGRAM--
FLINT PUBLIC SCHOOLS, SUMMARY REPORTS JULY 1, 1964 TO JUNE 30,
1965. Flint, Mich.: Flint Public Schools, 1965. (ED 002 396)

> One-page reports are presented, summarizing each of the projects
> in the Mott Program for the Flint Public Schools--workshops and
> visitations, adult education, graduate training, youth programs, the
> Mott Camp, recreation, "a better tomorrow for the urban child,"
> the personalized curriculum program, medical-dental health, inter-
> university clinical preparation, economics, and leadership.

Brown, Norman. LEARNING BY DOING. Chicago: Jewish Vocational
Service, 1971.

> The Chicago Jewish Vocational Service conducted a one-year pilot
> project (1970-71) in the Uptown Model City area of Chicago to
> develop a self-teaching work-readiness program for hard-core unem-
> ployed. The purpose of the project was to motivate the client by
> placing him in a position of responsibility, functioning between the
> foremen and other clients.

Coyle, H.F., Jr., et al. PROJECT TOTAL--TO TEACH ALL: AN INQUIRY
INTO THE DEVELOPMENT OF A MODEL FOR IDENTIFYING UNMET NEEDS
IN URBAN POST SECONDARY EDUCATIONAL OFFERINGS. FINAL REPORT.
Washington, D.C.: National Institute of Education, 1974. (ED 092 779)

Using the Akron, Ohio metropolitan area as the study area, the exploratory research Project Total is aimed at developing a generalizable model for analyzing urban adult educational needs, with disadvantaged adults receiving special attention.

Donaldson, O. Fred, and Davis, George A. "Teaching About Life in the City. VII. Geography, Social Action and the Black Community." NATIONAL COUNCIL FOR THE SOCIAL STUDIES YEARBOOK 42 (1972): 185-203.

Dordick, H. S. ADULT EDUCATION GOALS FOR LOS ANGELES: A WORKING PAPER FOR THE LOS ANGELES GOALS PROGRAM. Santa Monica, Calif.: RAND Corp., 1968.

The paper is concerned with adult education in the Los Angeles area. Future needs for specialized educational services that fall outside the formal educational structure of the state are discussed.

Drescher, Ruth. HEAD START PARENT'S ADULT BASIC EDUCATION PROJECT, NEW YORK CITY. FINAL REPORT. Albany: New York State Department of Education, 1968. (ED 018 761)

This book discusses a 100-hour education project which attempted to raise the educational level of parents of Head Start children in New York City during July and August 1967. None of the 1,488 registrants read beyond the eighth-grade level, most were non-English-speaking, and 38 percent were native born.

Friedman, Burton D. "Emphasizing the Urban in Urban Education." PHI DELTA KAPPAN 52 (March 1971): 425-26.

Problems in urban education stem from problems in urban living.

INSTRUCTIONAL MATERIALS FOR URBAN SCHOOLS: A BIBLIOGRAPHY OF MULTI-ETHNIC TEXTBOOKS AND SUPPLEMENTARY MATERIALS. New York: American Educational Publishers, 1969. (ED 033 992)

More than 1,000 titles are listed in this bibliography of instructional materials for urban schools, based on information gathered from sixty publishers. The grade levels range from preschool to 12th grade and each citation indicates the appropriate grade. The citations are grouped under the following principal subject headings: business, guidance, health and physical education, home economics, language arts, mathematics, science, social studies, vocational education, and adult basic education.

Lang, Carroll L. "Community Education in the Los Angeles Metropolitan Area." COMMUNITY EDUCATION JOURNAL 3 (January 1973): 59-60.

The author surveys the nature of community education in the Los

Angeles area and examines specific programs in the area. Needs for community education are discussed and the future of community education is examined.

MacVicar, John A. DESCRIPTION AND EVALUATION OF THE PLAYROOM 81 PROJECT. Cambridge, Mass.: Harvard University, Center for Research and Development in Educational Differences, 1968. (ED 032 605)

Playroom 81 was a recreational program available to children in the Mission Hill Extension Housing Development in Roxbury, Massachusetts. It was operated by ten mothers, both black and white, indigenous to the project. An evaluation of the program showed that participants and community people felt that there should be more organization and structure as well as a clearer delineation of roles in order to be effective. Playroom 81 did increase the achievement expectations of group members and help them become more self-reliant.

Mattran, Kenneth J. "Adult English as a Second Language Program in Chicago." Paper given at the third annual TESOL convention, Chicago, Illinois, 7 March 1969. (ED 030 849)

The writer discusses the "superb" overall organization of the program, and offers suggestions for overcoming the weaknesses in the areas of methodology, curriculum structure and development (including specific English objectives), and teacher qualification and training.

Mendelsohn, Harold, et al. OPERATION GAP-STOP: A STUDY OF THE APPLICATION OF COMMUNICATIONS TECHNIQUES IN REACHING THE UNREACHABLE POOR. FINAL REPORT. Vol. 1. Denver: Denver University, 1968. (ED 024 788)

This report presents a pioneering effort in the use of television in bringing to a particular sub-population, the disadvantaged, the particular kinds of information which could dispel ignorance in certain key informational areas.

_____. OPERATION GAP-STOP: A STUDY OF THE APPLICATION OF COMMUNICATIONS TECHNIQUES IN REACHING THE UNREACHABLE POOR. FINAL REPORT. Vol. 2. Denver: Denver University, 1968. (ED 024 816)

This second volume is a compilation of appendixes, which includes the questionnaire, the scripts for the eight television programs, and promotional material used to conduct the project.

Meyer, Sister Jean. "Reading Improvement for Urban-Area Adults." JOURNAL OF READING 14 (December 1970): 183-86.

Curriculum Development

Nesbitt, Charles. "Designing Relevant Programs for Urban Black Adults." ADULT LEADERSHIP 22 (January 1974): 249-52.

An established set of criteria for developing adult basic education programs for black adults in urban areas is needed. A reported Delphi study resulted in twelve recommended criteria which are described.

Peters, John M., and Gordon, R. Susan. ADULT LEARNING PROJECTS: A STUDY OF ADULT LEARNING IN URBAN AND RURAL TENNESSEE. Knoxville: University of Tennessee, 1974. (ED 102 431)

An extension of Alan Tough's original research on adult learning activities, the study surveyed large populations in rural and urban Tennessee to analyze learning patterns of adults engaged in learning projects.

Randolph, H. Helen. URBAN EDUCATION BIBLIOGRAPHY: AN ANNOTATED LISTING. New York: Center for Urban Education, 1968. (ED 024 474)

This annotated review of literature brings together publications concerning urban education, from September 1964 through December 1965.

Rosner, Joan, et al. PEOPLE AND CITIES: THE ENVIRONMENT AND SOCIETY. ADULT BASIC EDUCATION. Albany: New York State Education Department, Bureau of Continuing Education Curriculum Development, 1974. (ED 092 675)

The manual is designed to provide instructors in adult basic education with discussion and activities materials which treat the subject of environment and society. Each of the three topics ("People and Their Needs," "Understanding the City," and "Improving the City Environment") is comprised of objectives, background information for the instructor, suggested activities, and student worksheets.

Whipple, James B., et al. LIBERAL EDUCATION RECONSIDERED: REFLECTIONS ON CONTINUING EDUCATION FOR CONTEMPORARY MAN. NOTES AND ESSAYS ON EDUCATION OF ADULTS, 60. Syracuse, N.Y.: Syracuse University, Publications Program in Continuing Education, 1965. (ED 027 460)

These four essays are the final papers of staff members of the Center for the Study of Liberal Education for Adults; their theme is that liberal education embodies a concern for man rather than things.

Section D

SYNERGY AMONG INSTITUTIONS AND ORGANIZATIONS

Abbott, William. "Work in the Year 2001." THE FUTURIST 11 (February 1977): 26-31.

Technological breakthroughs will continue to change the world of work in the years ahead. But the workplace may be affected even more by the continuing revolutions in values, consciousness, knowledge, and equality. These changes, according to the author, are already transforming labor unions and universities, and have brought about an unusual alliance of big business, big labor, and big government.

APPENDIX. (NEIGHBORHOODS AND NEIGHBORHOOD CENTERS). Washington, D.C.: National Commission on Urban Problems, 1968.

Prepared in cooperation with the National Federation of Settlements and Neighborhood Centers, this report contains information on the rise of community schools in urban public education, neighborhood health centers, churches in the inner city, cooperatives and credit unions, neighborhood-based job training and placement programs, employment of nonprofessionals, urban observatories, and specific examples of various neighborhood service and development centers.

BALTIMORE METROPOLITAN AREA LIBRARY STUDY. RECOMMENDED LONG-RANGE WORK PROGRAM. Baltimore, Md.: Regional Planning Council, 1970.

Librarians in the Baltimore Metropolitan area have recognized the need to develop, on a cooperative basis, a region-wide planning, coordinating, and decision-making process. The report outlines a long-range work program, consisting of a series of research efforts which, when implemented, will supply the basic components of the desired planning process.

CALL AND COMMITMENT: ACTION TO ALLEVIATE CIVIL DISORDER AND ELIMINATE SOCIAL AND ECONOMIC INJUSTICE. National Governor's Conference. Advisory Committee on Federal-State-Local Relations. Washington, D.C.: 1967.

This conference resulted in a new commitment by states toward urban areas and the establishment of a checklist of important urban programs. Appearing on that list were: order and respect for law, full participation by all people in the process of government, physical rehabilitation of blighted areas, improved educational and employment opportunities, and full availability of effective service to the individual.

Cassel, Russell N. "A Proposed Experimental Secondary School Leadership Training and Development Program for Milwaukee." ADULT LEADERSHIP 19 (February 1971): 251, 275.

This proposal describes the plans, organization, and means for implementation of a leadership training and development program for the public and private high schools in Milwaukee. The program seeks to unite the senior high school, the home or family of a student, and the community in a mutually-cooperative effort for the identification, training, and development of local youth leadership.

Cave, William M., and Parsons, Thomas S. TOWARD A THEORY OF HOME, SCHOOL, AND COMMUNITY INTERRELATIONS. Ann Arbor: University of Michigan, n.d. (ED 020 526)

This theory of the community school program is presented through a detailed discussion of urban trends. The authors describe the historical prevalence of the economic and educative functions of families, and the effects of urbanization on those functions.

COMMUNITY FACILITIES INVENTORY: LIBRARIES, HOSPITALS, HIGHER EDUCATION FACILITIES. Baltimore, Md.: Regional Planning Council, 1967.

The report provides an inventory of existing libraries, higher education institutions (junior colleges, universities, etc.), and hospitals in the region, as well as a description of their planned expansion. The report also sets forth agency responsibilities and interrelationships necessary for planning these facilities.

Coyle, H.F., Jr., et al. PROJECT TOTAL--TO TEACH ALL: AN INQUIRY INTO THE DEVELOPMENT OF A MODEL FOR IDENTIFYING UNMET NEEDS IN URBAN POST SECONDARY EDUCATIONAL OFFERINGS. FINAL REPORT. Akron, Ohio: Akron University, Center for Urban Studies, 1973. (ED 092 779)

Using the Akron, Ohio metropolitan area as the study area, the exploratory research Project Total (To Teach All) is aimed at developing a generalizable model for analyzing urban adult educational needs, with disadvantaged adults receiving special attention. A primary purpose of the Project Total study is the collection of data for use in planning and coordinating postsecondary programs serving the needs of the urban disadvantaged.

Griffith, William S. "Synergy in Urban Relationships--Public School Adult Education, Community Colleges, and Community Education." Paper presented at the National Association for Public Continuing and Adult Education Conference, Chicago, Illinois, 6 November 1975. (ED 118 969)

> The presentation reviews selected developments in interorganizational cooperation and coordination at the local, state, and national levels in order to provide a basis for identifying major questions and issues faced by the National Council of Urban Administrators of Adult Education (NCUAAE) as they strive for synergy in adult education.

Hansen, Dean Maurice. "Avenues of Cooperation Between Three State Agencies Responsible for Post High School Education." Ph.D. dissertation, University of Florida, 1974.

> The problematic objective of this study was to identify and analyze the various avenues of interstate cooperational relationships emerging between three selected state administrative agencies regarding their increasingly overlapping responsibilities in educational programs beyond high school.

Miklich, James. "A Study of the Need for Agency Cooperation in Planning Coordination of Recreational Programs Among Four Recreational Agencies in Flint, Michigan." Ph.D. dissertation, University of Michigan, 1975.

> The major purpose of this study was to examine the perceived conflict and cooperation that existed between four recreational agencies who offered similar types of programs. An attempt was also made to determine the need for greater cooperation among agencies based on the perceived conflict between them.

Rogers, William C. "Needed for Citizenship Education: Urban Affairs Centers." ADULT LEADERSHIP 13 (April 1965): 315-16, 338.

> This author advocates the establishment of a one-stop center for adult citizenship education about urban affairs.

Rogers, William C., and Anderson, Dorothy. "How a True Life Urban Affair Started in Adult Leadership and What Happened Later." ADULT LEADERSHIP 19 (November 1970): 151-54.

> Believing that the problems of the cities were the most pressing American domestic questions during the last decades of the twentieth century, the University of Minnesota established a multipurpose, one-stop, educational center for adults interested in urban affairs.

Smith, Harold K. "A Plan for Developing a Program of Adult Education to Meet the Needs of a Local Community." Ed.D. dissertation, Rutgers, State University, 1968.

> Using local and national data, this study examined adult education

program offerings in East Orange, New Jersey, potential participants' needs and interests, and program needs reported by business
and industrial leaders. A plan was proposed for an appropriate
community-wide program.

A STUDY OF EDUCATIONAL COMPONENTS OF COMMUNITY ACTION PRO-
GRAMS. Silver Spring, Md.: Computer Applications, Education and Training
Department, 1969.

The general purpose of the study was to produce an organized body
of descriptive information about Community Action Agencies educational activity. The study was designed to gather information which
would focus upon a comparison between CAA educational activities
and specified CAP goals.

ADDENDUM

PART I, SECTION A

Levine, Daniel U., and Meyer, Jeanie Keeny. "Desegregation and White En-
rollment Decline in a Big-City School District." In THE FUTURE OF BIG-CITY
SCHOOLS, edited by Daniel U. Levine and Robert J. Havighurst, pp. 55-69.
Berkeley, Calif.: McCutchan, 1977.

> This is a summary and assessment of materials and arguments deal-
> ing with white flight from public schools. After noting that the
> issue has been temporarily settled, the authors present original re-
> search that such withdrawal has occurred in a large midwestern
> school district.

Orfield, Gary. "Policy Implications of Research on White Flight in Metropolitan Areas." In THE FUTURE OF BIG-CITY SCHOOLS, edited by Daniel U.
Levine and Robert J. Havighurst, pp. 70-84. Berkeley, Calif.: McCutchan,
1977.

> This chapter provides background information concerning white
> flight issues in the context of metropolitan development. Particu-
> lar emphasis is placed on interrelationships between desegregation
> policies in education and housing.

Wegmann, Robert G. "Desegregation and Resegregation: A Review of the Re-
search on White Flight From Urban Areas." In THE FUTURE OF BIG-CITY
SCHOOLS, edited by Daniel U. Levine and Robert J. Havighurst, pp. 11-54.
Berkeley, Calif.: McCutchan, 1977.

> This chapter reviews and analyzes the literature on desegregation
> and resegregation in urban schools and neighborhoods. He also
> includes a list of tentative conclusions and recommendations for
> achieving stable and constructive integration in big-city schools
> and neighborhoods.

Addendum

PART I, SECTION B

Clayton, Marian S. "Success Story of an Inner-City School." TODAY'S EDUCATION 65 (September-October 1976): 43-46.

> This article describes how an inner-city high school was improved by placing emphasis on reading and writing skills and their practical application in other courses, the development of a curriculum which was based on the real interests of students, and the encouragement of parents to be active in school and the community.

Cook, J. Marvin. "The D.C. Schools' Plan for Systemwide Achievement." EDUCATIONAL LEADERSHIP 35 (November 1977): 114-117.

> Cook describes the steps taken by the Washington, D.C. system to prepare them for the establishment of a competency-based educational program. It is a K-12 plan which focuses on monitoring student achievement of specific measurable competencies.

Estes, Nolan. "Using the R & D Approach in Improving Urban Education." EDUCATIONAL LEADERSHIP 34 (January 1977): 264-67.

> This is a report of how educators in Dallas, Texas, use context evaluation to help direct changes in instructional systems, materials, and methodology.

Eubanks, Eugene E., and Levine, Daniel U. "Jesse Jackson's PUSH Program for Excellence in Big City Schools." In THE FUTURE OF BIG-CITY SCHOOLS, edited by Daniel U. Levine and Robert J. Havighurst, pp. 218-34. Berkeley, Calif.: McCutchan, 1977.

> These authors analyze a program which was developed by Jesse Jackson to improve teaching and learning conditions in big-city schools. Basic ideology, components of the program, and critical issues are addressed.

Gibbons, Maurice. "Eleusis: The Secondary School Ideal." PHI DELTA KAPPAN 57 (June 1976): 655-60.

> This model is an attempt to integrate a number of developments into a new form of secondary education with a distinctive purpose, process, and context that will have a powerful and beneficial influence on the maturation of adolescents and their transition to adulthood.

Havighurst, Robert J., and Levine, Daniel U. "Instructional Improvement in Inner-City Schools." In THE FUTURE OF BIG-CITY SCHOOLS, edited by Daniel U. Levine and Robert J. Havighurst, pp. 235-46. Berkeley, Calif.: McCutchan, 1977.

This chapter assesses the instructional improvement in big- city schools in general and in inner-city schools in particular. They conclude that encouraging progress is being made in at least some locations.

PART I, SECTION C

Ciminillo, Lewis M. "Problems and Opportunities at an Urban Campus: A Professional Semester in Secondary Education." COLLEGE STUDENT JOURNAL 9 (April 1975): 135-40.

Indiana University Northwest is placing its teacher students program in the schools and communities where its students eventually will be employed. The professional semester is a competency-based program organized into a number of modules which are planned to develop different skills.

Lutz, Frank W., and Ramsey, Margaret A. PROBLEMS IN TRAINING AND UTILIZING URBAN EDUCATION LEADERSHIP. University Park: The Pennsylvania State University, 1975. (ED 109 737)

This is a report of positions expressed by teachers and administrators on the university-urban district cooperative leadership program carried out by Pennsylvania State University and the Philadelphia school district.

Peelle, Carolyn Curtiss. "A New Design for Higher Education: The UMass Center for Urban Education." PHI DELTA KAPPAN 56 (February 1975): 399-402.

The Center for Urban Education proposes that higher education become a change agent that works closely with local schools and communities. Emphasis is placed on curricula for diverse populations, inservice training, upward mobility, career training, and dialogues between diverse cultures and different races.

Rath, Ruth S. "General Semantics for Inner-City Teachers: A Summer Course." A REVIEW OF GENERAL SEMANTICS 31 (September 1974): 317-24.

The author describes a summer session workshop for inner-city teachers who wished to improve their professional performance of their teacher-student relationships.

Shoop, Robert J., and Schisler, Bryan L. "Community Education: Implications for Teacher Training." JOURNAL OF THOUGHT 11 (April 1976): 153-58.

In addition to discussing the alienation that has developed between the community and the public, the authors outline what should be the philosophy of community education and then discuss how this should be built into teacher training programs.

Addendum

WEST DALLAS TEACHER EDUCATION PROGRAM. Denton: North Texas State University, 1975. (ED 117 096)

> This program is a competency-based program to better prepare teachers for jobs in inner-city schools. The program utilizes a field-based, professional semester format to directly relate didatic instruction and clinical practice.

PART I, SECTION E

Campbell, Connie, and Levine, Daniel U. "Whitney Young Magnet High School of Chicago and Urban Renewal." In THE FUTURE OF BIG-CITY SCHOOLS, edited by Daniel U. Levine and Robert J. Havighurst, pp. 139-49. Berkeley, Calif.: McCutchan, 1977.

> This chapter identifies and illustrates some issues that should be considered by educators and planners in big cities when planning to implement a magnet school program. The information came from interviews with the teachers and administrators during the first year of operation of the school.

Finger, John A., Jr. "Policy Requirements for Successful Big-City Desegregation." In THE FUTURE OF BIG-CITY SCHOOLS, edited by Daniel U. Levine and Robert J. Havighurst, pp. 209-17. Berkeley, Calif.: McCutchan, 1977.

> This author discusses desegregation plans in several cities and identifies policies that he believes differentiate potentially successful from unsuccessful desegregation plans in the various cities.

Levine, Daniel U., and Campbell, Connie. "Developing and Implementing Big-City Magnet School Programs." In THE FUTURE OF BIG-CITY SCHOOLS, edited by Daniel U. Levine and Robert J. Havighurst, pp. 247-66. Berkeley, Calif.: McCutchan, 1977.

> The authors identify specific conclusions about policies and approaches for attaining desegregation and otherwise working to improve schools in big cities. One conclusion is that magnet schools may be helpful in improving racial and economic balance in city schools.

Levine, Daniel U., and Havighurst, Robert J. "Desegregation Policy, Urban Development, and the Future of Big-City Schools." In THE FUTURE OF BIG-CITY SCHOOLS, edited by Daniel U. Levine and Robert J. Havighurst, pp. 267-83. Berkeley, Calif.: McCutchan, 1977.

> Desegregation policies are outlined which particularly take into account the pervasive need to stop and reverse the growing phenomenon that has been occurring in many metropolitan areas.

PART II, SECTION A

Sole, Pat, and Wilkins, Arthur. "John Knox Village: Community Education and Retired Persons." COMMUNITY COLLEGE FRONTIERS 5 (February 1976): 13-14.

> The retirement community which has developed in the United States in the last several decades is a natural reservoir of students for continuing education programs. This article describes a successful program established in cooperation with a community college in an urban area.

PART II, SECTION C

Marshak, Robert E. "Problems and Prospects of an Urban Public University." DAEDALUS 104 (Winter 1975): 192-201.

> The author discusses the need for a complete reassessment of educational priorities for the urban university. Three goals are emphasized: inclusion of academically unprepared individuals in the university, development of academic curricula relevant to urban. problems, and development of research and service in areas related to the needs of the urban community.

Young, Barbara. "Higher Education for Welfare Mothers." SOCIAL WORK 22 (March 1977): 114-18.

> This article focuses on the impact higher education might have on the economic situation and personal growth of welfare mothers. The author reports the results of a study which confirmed that the large majority of welfare mothers are able to succeed academically and that this education provided them with improved possibilities for employment and increased satisfaction.

PART II, SECTION D

Evans, Robert L., and Kilgore, Alvan. "The Syracuse University Teaching Center: A Model for Preservice/Inservice Development." PHI DELTA KAPPAN 59 (April 1978): 539-41.

> This university has taken the lead in a collaborative effort involving the city school district, the local community, the teachers association, and the university. The Syracuse approach includes the development of three teaching centers whose primary aim is to integrate preservice and inservice education.

Addendum

PART III, SECTION D

Edwards, William L. "Public School Adult Education and the Importance of Community Agency Cooperation." COMMUNITY EDUCATION JOURNAL 5 (September–October) 1975): 9–10, 16.

> This author makes specific suggestions of ways to create working relationships and to establish rapport with the community.

Friedman, Abram. "Inter-Relationships: An Idea Whose Time Has Arrived." COMMUNITY EDUCATION JOURNAL 5 (September–October 1975): 11–13.

> Large urban areas present many problems which are unique to big cities. This article describes how the Los Angeles School District has developed relationships with outside groups in an effort to solve many of these problems.

Stewart, Brian. "A Community Adult Education Service." ADULT EDUCATION 49 (July 1976): 69–74.

> This article discusses the importance of the democratic process of involving people in thinking and making decisions about planning and playing an active part in the development and operation of services that will affect their daily lives.

APPENDIX

Listed below are significant organizations, journals, and information centers which were either used in the development of this bibliography or were included for their potential use to the reader. This list should not be considered exhaustive, but rather should be considered a starting place for individuals needing additional information.

I. ASSOCIATIONS

Association of Urban Universities
Jacksonville University
Jacksonville, Fla. 32211

Council of the Great City Schools
1707 H Street, N.W.
Washington, D.C. 20006

Council of Urban Administrators
National Association of Public Continuing and Adult Education
1201 Sixteenth Street, N.W.
Washington, D.C. 20036

New York City Urban Corps
250 Broadway
New York, N.Y. 10007

II. INFORMATION CENTERS

Clearinghouse for Adult Education and Lifelong Learning
Clearinghouse ADELL Information, Inc.
6011 Executive Boulevard
Rockville, Md. 20852

ERIC Clearinghouse in Career Education
The Center for Vocational Education
Northern Illinois University
204 Gurler School
DeKalb, Ill. 60115

ERIC Clearinghouse on Early Childhood Education
University of Illinois
College of Education
805 West Pennsylvania Avenue
Urbana, Ill. 61801

ERIC Clearinghouse on Higher Education
The George Washington University
One Dupont Circle, Suite 630
Washington, D.C. 20036

ERIC Clearinghouse on Junior Colleges
University of California, Los Angeles
Powell Library, Room 96
405 Hilgard Avenue
Los Angeles, Calif. 90024

ERIC Clearinghouse on the Disadvantaged
Columbia University, Teachers College, Horace Mann-Lincoln Institute
Box 40
525 West 120th Street
New York, N.Y. 10027

III. JOURNALS AND NEWSLETTERS

AUU Newsletter
Association of Urban Universities
Jacksonville University
Jacksonville, Fla. 32211

Education and Urban Society
Sage Publications
275 South Beverly Drive
Beverly Hills, Calif. 90212
(Interested in research or education as a social institution, and as an agent of
social change.)

IRCD Bulletin
Teachers College, Columbia University
Box 75
525 West 120th Street
New York, N.Y. 10027

AUTHOR INDEX

This index is alphabetized letter by letter.   Numbers refer to page numbers.
Indexed here are all authors, editors and compilers cited in this text.

A

Abbott, William   155
Abraham, Cleo   67
Abram, Robert E.   7
Ahlstrom, Winton M.   59
Alberty, Elsie J.   49
Allen, Anita F.   81
Allen, Hope E.   7
Allen, James E., Jr.   81
Alloway, David N.   81
Alverson, Hoyt S.   67
Amidon, Edmund J.   49
Anderson, Dorothy   157
Anderson, James J.   7
Anderson, Lowell D.   49
Arnez, Nancy L.   8, 67
Arnoff, Melvin   8
Arrington, J. Don   50
Arthur, Rita   8
Association of University Evening
   Colleges   113

B

Bailey, Stephen K.   50
Banyon, Shelia Doran   113
Baptiste, Hansom P., Jr.   50, 127
Barnes, Jarvis   8
Barney, William J., Jr.   81
Barrett, Donald N.   9

Barth, Roland S.   113
Bauer, Raymond   65
Belasco, James A.   20, 86
Bell, Peter   113
Berdow, John Richard   113
Bernert, Roman A.   127
Bernstein, Abraham   50
Berry, Gordon L.   109
Bess, Lorraine J.   50, 127
Bessent, Hattie   9
Bessent, Wailand   136
Best, Gilmary   128
Blanchard, Walter J.   68
Booms, Bernard   82
Bosley, Lenora   57
Bossone, Richard M.   50
Bottomly, Forbes   82
Bouchard, Ruth Ann   9
Bowles, Gladys K.   3
Bowman, Garda   128
Braverman, Miriam   9
Brazziel, William F.   113
Bremer, John   10
Brictson, Robert C.   111, 112
Briggs, Albert A.   68
Briggs, Larry   151
Broadbelt, Samuel   68
Brown, Norman   151
Brown, Roscoe C., Jr.   68
Bruker, R.M.   147
Brummit, Huston   10

Author Index

Author Index

Author Index

Author Index

TITLE INDEX

This index is alphabetized letter by letter. Numbers refer to page numbers. Lengthy titles are sometimes shortened. Indexed here are titles to all books, pamphlets, series, articles, dissertations, papers, and reports cited in this text.

D

E

Title Index

SUBJECT INDEX

This index is alphabetized letter by letter.   Underlined page numbers refer to main areas within the subject.

Subject Index

Subject Index

Subject Index

to Read Project
National Vocational-Technical Teacher
    Education Seminar (1968) 102
Natural science. See Science
Negroes. See Blacks
Neighborhoods
    educational associations and organi-
        zations in 69, 70, 71-72,
        78-79
    manpower and education programs
        in 16
    services and development centers
        in 155
    student guides to New York 4
    See also Community and college;
        Community and school
Neighborhood Youth Corps 28
    use of enrollees as tutors 12-13
Newark, N.J.
    community control of education in
        69, 73-74
    tutoring programs in 43
New Haven, Conn.
    community control of education in
        73
    educational failure in 67
    education of gifted students in 29
New Haven Community Action
    Coalition 73
New Jersey
    adult education in 149
    educational goals in 78
    education in 45
    See also East Orange, N.J.;
        Newark, N.J.
New Orleans
    adult education in 147
    science programs in 48
New York City 21, 85, 91
    adult education in 115, 152
    agricultural education in 11
    bilingual-bicultural programs in 18
    community control of education in
        72
    educational innovations in 83
    evaluation of educational programs
        in 17-18
    Headstart programs in 9
    High Horizons project in 41
    platoon schools in 92

school decentralization in 97
special education in 19
student guides to neighborhoods of
    4
teacher and paraprofessional train-
    ing in 57-58
teacher employment practices in
    53-54, 63
Title III projects in 35
See also Brooklyn, N.Y.
New York State 40-41, 45, 81
    reading programs in 39
    Urban Education Quality Incentive
        Program 18-19
    See also Buffalo, N.Y.; Rensselaer
        County, N.Y.; Rochester, N.Y.
Northeastern Illinois University,
        teacher training programs at
        52, 130
Northern Colorado, University of,
        Inner City Teacher Education
        Program 56-57, 133
Northern Illinois University, communi-
        cation skills programs at 125
Northern Virginia Pilot Project in
        Community Education 110
North Texas State University, West
        Dallas Teacher Education
        Program 141
Nursery schools
    Montessori method in 39
    value of 10
    See also Day care centers
Nutrition, in preschool programs 35

O

Oakland, Calif., vocational educa-
    tion in 46
Occupational education. See Career
    education; Vocational train-
    ing and education
Ohio. See Akron, Ohio; Cleveland,
    Ohio; Columbus, Ohio; Dayton,
    Ohio
Ohio State University, teacher train-
    ing programs at 49
Oklahoma State Department of Voca-
    tional and Technical Education
    139

Subject Index

models of 78
performance–objective programs in 21
readiness programs in 18–19
television in 27
See also Nursery schools; Project Headstart
Primary Education Project (PEP) 46
Principals
attitudes toward decentralization 65–66
need to assume leadership roles 78
Private schools 84
mathematics in 18
special education services in 19
Title I evaluation in 19
See also Parochial schools
Problem children, programmed tutoring for 12–13. See also Behavior
Programmed learning 47
for the behaviorally disordered 12–13
Project Assist 38
Project FICSS. See Focus on Inner City Social Studies
Project Follow Through, bibliography 30
Project Headstart 9, 22, 33
bibliography 30
evaluation of 35
parents of children in 152
See also Preschool education
Project Total—To Teach All 114–15, 151–52, 156
Property tax 74
Providence, R.I., community control of education in 68
Providence Educational Center (PEC), St. Louis, Mo. 38
Psychology, study and teaching of 117–18. See also Educational psychology
Public administration, continuing education in 106, 119
Public opinion in education 75
Public welfare. See Social welfare
Puerto Ricans
migration of to central–city areas 4
preschool education of 12

training of educators to teach 132
Purdue University, student–teacher attitude questionnaire of 138

Q

Queens College, teacher training programs at 62

R

Race
academic achievement and 71
composition of in the aged population 5
in education 15, 54, 73–74, 75, 77, 84, 90, 91, 92, 94, 139
imbalance of in urban college employment 4
in intelligence testing 23
problems of 88
quotas of in education 36
study of relations 103
See also Ethnicity; Minority groups; names of racial groups (e.g. Blacks)
Reading skills 139
of the culturally deprived 31
of dropouts 37
evaluation of programs of 8–9, 160
motivation in 9–10, 85, 160
study and teaching of 19, 24, 25, 30, 31, 33, 39, 42, 45, 47, 59, 71
in adult education 153–54
in elementary education 14–15, 16, 40
parental involvement in 68–69
in secondary education 17, 45, 160
by television
tutoring in 12–13, 15
teacher training for 45, 52, 58, 60–61
testing of 42
See also Phonetics
Reading skills centers 13–14, 15, 30, 47
Reasoning abilities, development of in disadvantaged students 20

Subject Index